TARTAN + TWEED

COMPASS:
TO TATE LIVERPOOL'S
SPRING PROGRAMME
£1
TATE

TARTAN + TWEED

Caroline Young / Ann Martin

CONTENTS

previous page Inspiration images collected by Joanne McDonnell, Urgha Loom Shed.

left Bobbins of yarn ready to be made into Harris Tweed.

THE STORY OF TARTAN

A silk velvet tartan dress worn by Queen Victoria as a teenager around 1835, when tartan was highly fashionable.

The uniform of the Royal Company of Archers. The society was originally formed to promote archery as a sport in Edinburgh and in 1713 a new all-tartan uniform was created.

Tartan is the fabric of a nation, an icon of Scottish history and identity, with countless meanings attached – regimental, rebellious and with a sense of belonging. It's also one of the most versatile of fabrics. It is warm and waterproof, and the infinite variety of patterns, or setts, lend themselves to creating a unique uniform or brand. But it is generally accepted that, while there is evidence of wearing tartan in Scotland in ancient times, and that plaid was the universal costume of Highlanders from the sixteenth century to the Battle of Culloden in 1746, the concept of clans having their own traditional tartan is a fairly recent one.

In the Middle Ages plaid was a large piece of patterned cloth which acted as a functional item of clothing and as bedding, and could be worn in a versatile way. The pattern of the cloth would eventually be known as tartan, and over time the word 'plaid' would be used to describe the check pattern, particularly in North America.

A variety of factors in the nineteenth century, including industrialization and a romantic rewriting of Scottish history, led to the classification of clan tartan as it became a mass-manufactured product. The Battle of Culloden, the formation of Highland regiments and mass migration as a result of the Highland Clearances in the eighteenth and nineteenth centuries all played a part in a cultural shift that led to tartan becoming a global fabric. The vast majority of tartans do not predate the Battle of Culloden and, with the tartan authority registering 8,000 tartans and counting, most are considered to be modern designs.

All woven fabrics are made from the warp and the weft: the warp is the thread stretched out on the loom, and the weft is the thread that is woven through it. In tartan the colour stripes are provided in a series of numbers to indicate how the sett will form with different-coloured threads. These are replicated on the warp and the weft, to form tiles. As more colours are introduced to the weave, an infinite number of setts can be produced. The greater the number of colours used the more muted the overall tartan becomes as the tones are mixed together. The simplest tartan is the Rob Roy or Buffalo check, as it uses just red and black, creating only three shades in total.[1]

THE ORIGINS OF TARTAN

Going back to tartan's ancient origins, it's clear that checked fabric was not unique to Scotland. Ancient pieces of woven twill, with two or more different yarns woven to form a striped cloth, have been excavated around the world. The chequered Gerum Cloak was discovered in a peat bog in Sweden in 1920, and is believed to date from 360 BC to 100 BC, while the Tarim mummies found in China's Taklamakan desert, believed to date from 1800 BC to first century BC and to be Indo-European, were dressed in a vibrant tartan-style cloth. These have links to the Hallstatt salt caves in Austria, where checked woven cloth dating from

the Iron Age was discovered, and believed to be from 1500 BC to 350 BC. These textiles were twills made from bright coloured wool and were woven on looms.[2]

Scotland's oldest piece of tartan is known as the Falkirk tartan, and is believed to date from around AD 230. It was discovered in 1934, stuffed into the mouth of a pot containing a large collection of Roman coins. It had a simple check with two shades of brown, and was a peasant cloth – likely to have been worn by shepherds to keep warm.[3]

The challenges of Scotland's landscape and climate influenced how the culture of the Highlands developed, and the Picts, Britons, Gaels and the Norse fought for control of the land. In the *Aeneid*, written between 29 BC and 19 BC, Virgil referenced the Picts' clothing – 'their cloaks are striped and shining'[4] – indicating they wore a patterned fabric, like that of the Falkirk tartan, and this is believed to have been a cloak worn over a tunic with bare legs. A Norse king called Magnus Barelegs (also referred to as Magnus Barefoot) fought in the Crusades and there's reference in a letter to King Henry VIII that the Highlanders were called 'redshanks' because of their exposed legs.[5]

A good account of the use of plaid was recorded in a book called *Letters from a Gentleman in the North of Scotland*, written in 1726 by Edward Burt, a surveyor under General Wade who ordered roads to be built in the Highlands after the first Jacobite rebellion some ten years earlier. Burt described the Highlanders as being frequently wet from the rain and boggy landscape, how they would use their plaid as a cloak and as a blanket, and how the perspiration would soak into the fabric, resulting in a 'filthy smell'. They would also dip a corner of the plaid in water and envelop themselves tightly within their plaid to sleep on the ground: 'where the wet and the warmth of their bodies make a steam like that of a boiling kettle'.[6]

Before the Battle of Culloden, plaid was seen as barbaric and licentious by those outside the Highlands, and it was often insinuated that tartan allowed the Highlanders to disguise themselves in the heather to rob and steal. The Revd Thomas Morer in 1692 said 'lowlanders say, being thieves, these plaids cover stolen booty',[7] while Burt wrote about the prejudice in other parts of Britain that tartan encouraged 'an idle life in lying upon the heath' and that it 'serves to cover them in the night when they lie in wait among the mountains, to commit their robberies and depredations; and is composed of such colours as altogether, in the mass, so nearly resemble the heath on which they lie'.[8]

TARTAN ETYMOLOGY AND TRADITIONS

The word 'tartan' is likely to have derived from the French *tiretaine* or *tertaine* and the Spanish *tiritana*, which is a blend of linen and wool. The word was more common in the lowlands[9] and was first documented in print in a treasurer's record for James III in 1471,

A woman weaving Royal Stewart tartan on a loom at the Wilson and Glenny mill at Hawick, Scottish Borders in 1950.

when he ordered 'tartane' for his clothing. However, the Gaelic word *breacan* described a piece of patterned cloth that could be wrapped around the body – with *breac* meaning speckled. *Breacan* was mentioned in a late eleventh-century letter by the bishop of St Andrews as '*diversis coloribus vestes*', while John Taylor described Highland dress in 1618 as being made of short hose 'made of warm stuffe of divers (diverse) colours they call tartan'.[10]

Weaving coloured checks was easier to do than dyeing whole pieces of fabric with limited equipment, and it was also an expressive form of design with different colour combinations possible, and where the checks were chosen as a matter of personal taste. Upright looms were traditionally used to weave tartan, where warp threads were fixed along a wooden frame and held taut by weights at the base. Although the flying shuttle was invented in England in 1733, it took time to filter up to the Highlands, but it meant that looms became horizontal, and pedals allowed the hand to be free to throw a shuttle from side to side. The spinning wheel was introduced in the early eighteenth century, with an early version known as a muckle wheel.[11]

There were many traditions and customs when it came to production of tartan, one of them being the 'waulking' of the cloth, where women manipulated the cloth in time to their singing to pull and stretch it. Women

left This 1821 illustration from *Costume of the Original Inhabitants of the British Islands*, depicting 'Hibernian male and female costume' is typical of the fascination at the time with ancient Scottish costume.

above A portrait of Lord Mungo Murray, son of first Marquess of Atholl, painted by John Michael Wright around 1683, depicting the sitter in a belted plaid dressed for hunting.

'I do not believe a word of the nonsense about every clan or name having a regular pattern which was undeviatingly adhered to.' Sir Walter Scott

of the household would weave their own everyday items such as blankets and shawls, likely to be coloured with vegetable dye and whatever they could afford, while professional weavers would be commissioned for special pieces and would use imported dyes to create vivid colours. However, early weaves such as the Falkirk tartan would have been naturally coloured – in blacks, browns and whites, corresponding with the colours from the sheep's wool.

Before the eighteenth century, wool came from a variety of now-extinct Highland sheep from which the wool could be plucked instead of shorn, and it was finer than the coarse wool of modern breeds. The Cheviot had a fine undercoat and a coarser overcoat which could be utilized for creating either a rough 'hard' tartan with finely combed yarn from dense wool, or else a finer fabric, which would be more expensive. The mineral content of water had an effect on how vibrant and strong the colour would turn out, depending on the hardness of the wool – some were more resistant to colour than others.[12]

As the Renaissance swept through Western Europe from the fifteenth century there was a flourish of style, and tartan was the Highland response to this more fashion-conscious era with a desire to wear the most vivid, eye-catching colours. Early portraits such as that of Highland chief Lord Mungo Murray, by John Murray Wright in 1683, depict the sitter's outfits at their very best, using a variety of different-coloured tartans for the plaid, stockings and trews.

TARTAN COLOURINGS

Being the most expensive and brightest of dyes, red was one of the most sought-after colours for tartans, and the majority of portraits also depict costumes of red tartan, indicating wealth and good taste. In Gaelic song, clothing was often praised for its vivid colours, particularly if that colour was red. Hugh Cheape noted: 'In the same way as it is now, in the fifteenth and sixteenth century, what you wore could be an object of praise, and the highest praise was given to those that had the brightest and reddest clothes, which was undoubtedly the most expensive.'[13]

The late James D. Scarlett, considered one of the authorities on the history of tartan, said: 'The cloth that came from Highland looms was hard and harsh, of great durability and often extremely fine woven. The colours were clear, bright and soft, altogether unlike the eye-searing brilliance or washed out dullness of modern tartans and the patterns too, tended to be bolder and more clearly defined. The result was a harmonious blend of colour and pattern worthy to be looked upon as an art form in its own right.'[14]

It is believed that, when tartan was handwoven, weavers used locally found dyes in minerals, vegetables and fruits such as bark, moss, heather, bracken, bog myrtle and ragwort. Urine could be mixed with lichens to react and form crimsons and purples, and the substances would be boiled for a long period of time to release the dye, and a metal fixer was then added.[15] It is a romantic notion, and one referenced by Lord Archibald Campbell in *Record of Argyll*: 'To seek the day the first lassie culled the first blueberry to dye the cloth of her lover; to seek the primeval man who first used bullock's blood to dye the splendid red used in some of the clan colours . . . they are older than the history of any costume that was ever written.'[16]

However, a comprehensive study by National Museums of Scotland that was carried out by Hugh Cheape and Anita Quye concluded that old tartan fragments commonly revealed the presence of insect dyes rather than vegetable dyes, indicating that Scotland imported exotic dyes from overseas – such as cochineal from South America and indigo from India – and that these became widely available through travelling traders and at markets across the country. Their study was initially carried out on a piece of tartan from a kilt said to have been worn by Bonnie Prince Charlie at the Battle of Culloden in 1746. Cheape and Quye noted that: 'The sett of the prince's tartan appeared to have an overcheck of red and yellow lines on a blue and green "ground". The colours of blue, derived from indigo, and red, derived from cochineal, were popular and fashionable colours in tartan in seventeenth and early eighteenth century Scotland.' They also discovered that yellow dyes in the analyzed samples were 'more often derived from native plants such as heather, bog myrtle and gorse and trees such as silver birch and willow, but dyestuffs from imported materials such as weld and old fustic were also found.'[17]

There has been some thought that colours of tartan were linked to areas where particular dyes were available. However, due to the trade links, different dyes weren't limited to a particular region. 'I much doubt the correctness of a theory that district and clan tartans were influenced by the supply of local-dye plants because most of those in general use are fairly widely distributed,' said researcher and curator Isabel Grant in her book *Highland Folk Ways*. But some of the earliest tartans were district tartans such as the Old Lochanar, the Lennox and the Huntley, which were designed by local weavers who developed a particular style and preference for certain colours.[18]

From the seventeenth century or earlier, clans differentiated from each other in battle with the sprig of a plant adorning their bonnet. Clan Donald and associate clans – MacAllisters, MacDonalds, MacIains and MacDonnells – wore heather; Clan MacFarlane and Clan MacAulay used cranberry; the Grants, MacGregors and MacKinnon were represented by pine; and gale, also known as bog-myrtle, was the symbol of the Campbells. Isabel Grant argued that it was this that differentiated clans rather than tartans. There was a saying after the Battle of Inverlochy in 1645 that 'the heather was above the gale', meaning that Clan Donald were victorious over the Campbells; however, there was no equivalent evidence that tartan was raised in victory.[19]

While tartan was predominantly worn by men for plaids and trews from the eighteenth century, prior to that women had worn the arisaid, which was a long checked plaid that could be draped over the head or pinned with

***left** The Order of Release 1746* by John Everett Millais from 1853, depicting a woman with her wounded husband as he is released from prison after the failure of the second Jacobite uprising.

right Crofters in their cottage in the Shetlands around 1910, with a spinning wheel in the centre of the room.

a large jewelled brooch in a Gaelic design or by a luckenbooth silver brooch. Wealthier women wore their arisaid with a silk lining and in bright, vivid colours. However, by the eighteenth century the arisaid had fallen out of fashion and women began to choose lowland-style clothing instead.[20]

THE BAN ON HIGHLAND DRESS

Following the Jacobite defeat at Culloden in 1746, the Act of Proscription 1746 was enforced. Clan chiefs were to appear before the local authority and swear an oath to 'never use tartan plaid, or any part of the Highland garb, and if I do so may I be accursed in my undertakings, family and property, may I never see my wife, nor children, nor father, mother, or relations, may I be killed in battle as a fugitive coward'.[21] Because tartan provided a visual sign of rebellion, preventing its use was a way to quash any future uprisings. Under proscription it would be extremely dangerous to wear tartan; Highlanders could be fined £15 or serve six months in prison, and if they were seen wearing tartan for a second time the punishment would be transportation to the colonies for seven years.

below Officers of the 42nd Royal Highland Regiment, known as the Black Watch, during the Crimean War, 1853–1856.

right A photograph of Afghan soldiers dressed in kilts, taken by John Burke in 1879. The Afghans were impressed with the fighting skills of the British Highland regiments and dressed in kilts in an attempt to instil within them similiar qualities.

As a result of this Act, the production of handwoven tartan all but disappeared in the Highlands, and the traditions and skills of weaving as well as many of the ancient recipes for dye were lost. By 1760 Highlanders were very unlikely to be reported for wearing tartan, and when the Act of Proscription was repealed in 1782 there was celebrating, particularly in areas of strong Jacobite support, such as Glengarry. But very few people brought out their old tartans; instead, they dressed in a combination of Highland and English dress, such as a bonnet and hose with fine doublets. Fishermen and crofters wore home-spun knitted jerseys in plain blues and browns, trousers and bonnets, which were more practical for their labour.[22]

THE RAISING OF HIGHLAND REGIMENTS

Despite the huge losses and eradication of the Highland way of life, Culloden had proved that the Highlanders were good warriors who would follow orders, and this encouraged Prime Minister William Pitt the Elder to raise Highland regiments to fight for the empire in France and North America. Between 1757 and 1761 nine regiments were raised and these soldiers in their tartan uniform became the heroes of the day, creating an image of the Scottish warrior in campaigns overseas.[23] Already after the 1715 Jacobite rising, six independent companies had been formed to help keep control in the Highlands. They acted as a version of military police, keeping an eye out for the 'black' trade of cattle theft, and they became known as the Black Watch. They wore a uniform tartan of dark green, blue and black, which would later be closely associated with the Campbell tartan, given that three of the six regiments were Campbell. The Campbells were known for their loyalty to the Hanoverian government, having infamously carried out orders for the execution of the MacDonalds at Glencoe in 1692.

According to Hugh Cheape, this dark green, blue and black tartan was chosen so as not to clash with the red jackets worn with the uniform, and perhaps because the colourings were to stand apart from the more popular red tartans worn by civilians. These tartans would later be personalized for the regiments as they were raised, so that Gordon had an overcheck of yellow while Mackenzie used overchecks of white and red, for example.[24]

There was a degree of classification with the tartans for Highland regiments as the wealthy landowners who were raising the regiments sought to develop an appropriate tartan for their troops, using the government tartan, or Black Watch, as a basis.

Despite the Act of Proscription, production of tartan actually increased between 1746 and 1782 because tartan was needed to supply the uniforms for these regiments. It was only in the Highlands that tartan had been banned, and during proscription it became quite fashionable in England, partly down to the intrigue of a banned fabric.[25]

As Scottish soldiers wore tartan, and wealthy landowners supported the raising of their regiments by wearing the tartan of the uniform, tartan became popular as military-wear. By the 1790s it became ultra-fashionable to pronounce a Highland connection and have a tartan created and woven. 'The frequency, length and prominence of the conflicts at the turn of the nineteenth century meant that military style infiltrated fashionable dress of men and women throughout Britain at an unprecedented level,' said Dr Sally Tuckett from the University of Glasgow.[26] Paris in 1815 was occupied by Scottish regiments and there was an allure about these kilted men. Magazine *La Belle Assemblee* in April 1815 reported that French women used tartan ribbons and handkerchiefs in support of these troops, harking back to the Auld Alliance between France and Scotland.

The demand for tartan became more pronounced following the visit of George IV to Edinburgh in 1822, when Sir Walter Scott turned the visit into a tartan show by encouraging Highland chiefs to turn up in full Highland dress. In the lead up to the king's visit, the city was swept up in 'tartanmania' with fabric merchants making a fast profit on their tartans. During this time, the firm of Romanes & Paterson, which had been founded in Edinburgh in 1815, stocked up on a wide range of tartan products such as tartan satins, shawls and handkerchiefs.[27]

CLASSIFYING TARTANS

Strict detailed classification of clan tartans essentially emerged at the beginning of the nineteenth century when the Highland Society in London, a patriotic society set up by Highlanders with the principal aim of supporting the economic recovery of the region, really pushed the idea of creating a record of clan tartans. With their sister branch in Edinburgh, they worked together to research the distinct culture of the Highlands including music, language and tartans.[28]

According to Hugh Cheape: 'The Highland Society set up a circular questionnaire to all clan chieftains, sixty or eighty individuals, asking what tartans they used – quite evident none had given much thought to it, as the idea of set tartans didn't really exist. We have evidence of how they responded – they all sent in pieces of tartan, which were bound in a book on clan tartan at the Highland Society of London, with listings compiled from 1810 to 1820 ... while the original collection of tartan samples was cut apart and rearranged in other books, there was enough of the fabric swatches left to give an idea of each tartan.'[29]

A contemporary sketch of George IV in Highland dress at the Palace of Holyrood, Edinburgh, by David Wilkie in 1822.

above Women in the mending room at the Wilson and Glenny tartan mill in Hawick, 1950.

opposite A Victorian dress in wool tartan, trimmed with dark green velvet, from around 1885.

Because of this desire to discover the ancient history of clan tartans, two brothers – the Sobieski Stuarts, claiming to be Bonnie Prince Charlie's grandsons – received a hero's welcome in Edinburgh when they arrived around 1830. They were invited to go up north and subsequently settled on an estate near Beauly, where they set themselves up as gurus on tartan and travelled the Highlands to meet important chieftains. Taking advantage of this thriving market for tartan, the Sobieski Stuarts meticulously produced documents with two versions of medieval manuscripts of tartan – *Vestiarium Scoticum* in 1842 and *The Costumes of the Clans* also in 1842 – which caused a huge stir.[30]

While their real identities are now known, and some historians have dismissed their stories as fanciful, Hugh Cheape believed their research to be valuable: 'In Uist, the Sobieski brothers recorded a remark that chief of Clan Ranald wore silk tartan from Barcelona which had a strong silk industry. So it's credible that Ranald got silk from Barcelona, and he might have asked for their red version, for example. So even if the Sobieskis did produce a fake manuscript, it was still fifteen years of valuable research.'[31]

MANUFACTURING AND MARKETING A FABRIC

With this fascination for tartan, and with a need for regiments to be outfitted, major tartan manufacturers such as William Wilson & Son of Bannockburn had

begun creating and naming tartans from a commercial point of view. When Wilson & Son first started producing tartans in their factory, around 1770, the setts were given names such as Hyland Tartan, Caledonian 1, Robin Hood or Meg Merrilees, but after George IV's 1822 visit, and with the powerful image of the clan chiefs in their tartans, Wilson & Son began changing the names of tartans to that of Scottish clans, partly as a marketing technique to sell more tartans. While the demand was there, they could keep on producing new setts for people to purchase. Meanwhile, also in 1822, they had opened the Royal George Mill, which covered more than three storeys and had a watermill, mechanized spinning and handloom weaving, so they could keep up with orders coming in from as far afield as Brazil, the United States and Jamaica.[32]

The market was insatiable for new tartan weaves and books documenting the history. In 1845 the writer James Logan and illustrator R.R. McIan created a book called *The Clans of the Scottish Highlands* containing romantic images and information on all the clan chieftains in apparently traditional Highland dress. There was a fanciful nature to it, as it wasn't known exactly what these clans would have worn, but the illustrations by McIan were widely replicated, creating the concept of the romantic Scottish warrior, and these illustrations are still reproduced to this day.[33]

While many Scots loved the idea of this fashion for tartan, others were cynical – they thought Scotland

Adverts by London North Eastern and London Midland & Scottish Railways to promote travel to the Highlands around 1930.

was turning into a stereotype where Highland culture was becoming representative of the whole country and history was being rewritten. Sir Walter Scott had been sceptical and had in 1825 written: 'I do not believe a word of the nonsense about every clan or name having a regular pattern which was undeviatingly adhered to.'[34]

By the mid-nineteenth century, tartan production had become fully mechanical, with the invention of power looms in textile factories around Kilbarchan near Glasgow and Comrie in Perthshire. Tartans became brighter and dressier for the fashion-conscious, while ancient versions were muted in tone to replicate the supposedly faded material of early, handwoven tartan. The hard tartan of dense twill became softer and there was a fashion for wearing tartan dresses in silk and velvet.

There's an example of a dress in the Royal Collection worn by a young Princess Victoria around 1835, which demonstrated this fashion. 'If you look at the fabric you can clearly see it is silk velvet and it's not tartan at all. But it's pretending to be tartan. And these types of fabric were probably woven in France and were incredibly fashionable about 1825 to 1840 across the continent,' said Caroline de Guitaut, curator of the exhibition *Fashioning a Reign*, by the Royal Collection Trust.[35] The Inverness Museum also has an example of a fine tartan gown worn for Queen Victoria's visit to Drummond Castle in 1842 by Lady Willoughby d'Eresby, daughter of James Drummond.

VICTORIAN ROMANTICISM

Tartan was sentimentalized further as nineteenth-century visitors to Scotland wished to take home tartan as a souvenir of their Highland travels. Taking the lead from Queen Victoria and her husband Albert, English aristocracy visited Scotland over the summer months for shooting, hunting and fishing. The arrival of the railway in Inverness in 1854 led to a boom in outdoor recreation, and Nairn, Strathpeffer and Dornoch became Highland resorts.[36] Ironically, while the Highland way of life was treated as a romance, crofters were being forcibly removed from their land under the Highland Clearances as wealthy landowners evicted their tenants so they could convert the land to sports estates or for industrial farming. A century earlier when the Act of Proscription 1746 had banned the wearing of tartan and the speaking of Gaelic, what resulted was a form of ethnic cleansing for those who couldn't speak English.

Early tartan souvenirs became all the rage for Victorians, with items such as snuff boxes, tea caddies, card cases and wooden buttons all decorated with tartan. Other products such as Walkers shortbread, Camp coffee and Scotch tape became synonymous with tartan through their advertising. Tartan in the twentieth century, as will be discussed in The Popularity of Tartan chapter (see page 52), became widespread – taking on many new meanings and symbols.

LMS
THE HIGHLAND GAMES
By CHRISTOPHER CLARK. R.I.
Mary, Queen of Scots, stood beneath the Hangman's Tree at Inveraray, to watch the very first Highland Games, in 1554. Still to-day they are held, every August and September, with stirring rivalry in hammer-throwing, caber-tossing, dancing and wrestling.
Come to the Cowal Games at Dunoon (with a thousand pipers marching!); to the Northern Meeting at Inverness, on the site of Macbeth's Castle; to Oban, Strathpeffer, Nairn or Crieff–to "Gatherings" of romantic splendour amid the purple of Scottish heather.
LNER

ROB ROY
LNER
WESTERN HIGHLANDS
LMS
IT'S QUICKER BY RAIL
FULL INFORMATION FROM ANY LNER OR LMS OFFICE OR AGENCY

THE HISTORY OF THE KILT

Illustration from around 1850 showing King Edward I (1239–1307) fighting the Scots.

Scottish bagpiper dressed in traditional red and black tartan kilt, hose and sgian dubh.

When we think of the kilt we think of Scotland, so entwined is this national dress within its country's heritage. Known around the world, the distinctive vertical and horizontal tartan check has become synonymous with bagpipes and brave gents. The kilt wearer is met with pride, intrigue and historical anecdotes of country and kin. Few other national costumes have such emotive meaning and, despite its conflicting history, the kilt stands strong as a stimulating symbol of Scotland's identity.

James Macpherson's poem 'Ossian' (1762) was largely responsible for casting the early Highland Scots as romantic heroes and preceded a lengthy literary heritage from Sir Walter Scott. 'It was MacPherson, rather than Sir Walter Scott, who first turned Highland clansmen into romantic warriors,' said historian Stuart Reid. 'In the process he also provided a culturally insecure Scotland with a highly distinctive creation myth and a romantic literary heritage firmly rooted not in the douce, respectable Lowlands of John Knox, David Hume and Adam Smith, or even in Scott's beloved wild borderland, but in the infinitely wilder Highlands.'[1]

More recently film-makers have championed the Highland hero with blockbusters *Highlander*, *Rob Roy* and *Braveheart* highlighting the ruggedly seductive appeal of the kilt and positioning the boisterous Scottish hero who defies authority and the elements at the forefront of public consciousness. Yet there is more to the kilt than is seen on screen. In fact it is so rich in history that the origins and references attributed to this native Scottish dress cover more than two thousand years. From the Romans who described ancient Celts as wearing 'striped' dress to the Victorians who championed tartan as the fashion *du jour*, the kilt has seen many guises and even survived several decades of decline when Highland dress was prohibited by the British government after the second Jacobite rebellion (see pages 19–20).

EARLY HISTORY

The origins of the kilt are much disputed with theories varying dramatically and discussions about the history of the kilt rife with disagreement. Early Irish stone carvings depicting men in knee-length garb have led to speculation that kilts were developed in Ireland, for example, and later imported by Scots. The early history is shrouded in myth and debate, and like any story passed from one to another, the story of the kilt has been privy to controversial embellishment and fabrication over the years. John Telfer Dunbar's conclusion that 'any attempt to fix its obscure origins precisely is undoubtedly foolish'[2] resonates with the current body of historical reference that is often thought to be ambiguous and contradictory; thus it is unlikely that the exact origins of the kilt will ever be conclusive. Yet there is merit in assessing the broad historical landscape and demonstrating the kilt's evolution over time, tracking its journey from rural dress to a modern badge of Scotland.

We do know that 1,000 years ago the kilt in its familiar form did not exist in the Scottish Highlands. The Highlanders or Gaels wore a 'leine' typically reaching to their knees and a semi-circular mantle known as the 'brat'. The 'trews' were worn underneath these loose garments and it is said they were adopted by the chieftains to mark their social distinction because they were largely impractical for everyday Highland life. Worn to the ankle, the origin of 'trews' is found in Ireland, where local dress mirrored that of the Scots Highlanders. While we don't typically associate shirts with Highland dress, most early references to native clothing refer to 'over-shirts' or tunics worn until the end of the sixteenth century by both sexes. By this time the 'leine' had evolved into a more flamboyant, full-sleeved garment often undyed but occasionally coloured with saffron, known as a 'Saffron Shirt'. A woollen wrap or 'plaid' was worn over the tunic to protect the wearer against the extreme Highland weather. Bishop Leslie wrote in 1578: 'They made also of linen very large shirts, with numerous folds and wide sleeves, which flowed abroad loosely to their knee. These, the rich coloured with saffron and other smeared with grease to preserve them longer clean among the toils and exercises of a camp'.[3]

If we are to accept the accounts of other sixteenth-century writers, it appears that tartan was not worn

'Any attempt to fix the kilt's obscure origins precisely is undoubtedly foolish.' John Telfer Dunbar

in relation to a specific clan at this time. It was the fabric's colour that identified social standing, with chiefs in coloured plaid and their clansmen in neutral brown. The Highlanders themselves preferred natural colours that allowed them to blend into their surrounding environment. In his myth-damning book *The Emperor's New Kilt*, Jan Andrew Henderson conceded that 'a range of clear bright colours was possible' but that the colours were nothing like modern tartan with 'varying shades pretty much out of the question'.[4]

By the seventeenth century fashions favoured fuller clothing with extensive layers that indicated wealth and status. Tartan fabric was gathered around the waist and belted, and known in Gaelic as the *fèileadh-mòr* (great wrap) or *breacan-an-fèileadh* (tartan wrap). The *fèileadh-mòr* was placed on the ground in pleats, and the wearer would wrap the edges of the fabric around his stomach and secure it using a heavy leather belt. Once standing he would typically drape the excess material around one shoulder and fasten with a pin. Women too wore the plaid (later the arisaid) reaching from their shoulders to the feet and secured with a pin, much like the male alternative.

Martin Martin's 1690s' account of the plaid – 'wore only by the men is made of fine wool, the threads as fine as can be made of that kind. It consists of divers colours: and there is a great deal of ingenuity required in sorting colours so as to be agreeable to the nicest fancy'[5] – is often referenced as evidence of early tartan and used to give chronological significance to the timeline of kilt development. However, it is unclear whether tartan was in regular production at this time, given the significant cost involved in making the cloth.

THE KILT

Unlike the plaid, kilts required just a single width of material, making them more economical and wearable, and by the end of the eighteenth century plaids were no longer the norm. Occasionally a small section of fabric was worn hanging from the left shoulder in a similar shape to the belted plaid. Replacing the plaid was the first iteration of the kilt - simple folds brought together with a belt and free-flowing lower fabric that nodded to the plaid that had come before.

Some historians suggest that Edward Burt, a chief surveyor for Highland roads, was the first to mention the word 'kilt' – or 'quelt' as it was then known – in a letter to an English friend. Written between 1725 and 1726, Burt's letters described the garment similar to the belted plaid, the kilt 'set in folds and girt round the waist to make of it a short petticoat that reaches half-way down the thigh, and the rest is brought over the shoulders and then fastened.'[6]

It is widely believed that Quaker Thomas Rawlinson, who owned an iron factory in the Scottish Highlands, modified the clothing of his workers in the

A young man sewing the back pleats of a kilt to canvas, 1952.

eighteenth century because the traditional *fèileadh-mòr* was too hot to wear in his smelting factory. He reportedly commissioned a local tailor in Inverness to cut the plaid in half, separating the pleated section from the draping, stitching the pleats at the back and adding flat aprons at the front secured with a belt, which became the familiar kilt shape we know today. Local chief Ian MacDonnell, who had rented his land to Rawlinson, apparently adopted the *fèileadh-beag* (little kilt) and encouraged his clansmen to do the same.

British historian Hugh Trevor-Roper supported the notion that Rawlinson was responsible for the kilt, challenging the idea that it was developed over time: 'We may thus conclude that the kilt is a purely modern costume, first designed, and first worn, by an English Quaker industrialist; and it was bestowed by him on the Highlanders, not in order to preserve their traditional way of life, but to ease its transformation: to bring them off the heath and into the factory.'[7] Nick Fiddes, owner of DC Dalgliesh, the world's only hand-crafted tartan mill, concludes that 'locating the authentic tradition of the kilt is an impossible conquest. Since few ideas are truly original, it is likely that the kilt arrived simultaneously amongst a variety of social groups. As its true origins are lost to myth we focus our attentions on the modern kilt story that is still being invented and shaped today.'[8]

It's clear that in the absence of concrete evidence the ferocious debate about the origins of the kilt will

left In this 1749 painting attributed to William Mosman, the sons of Sir Alexander Macdonald of Macdonald are shown wearing tartan as an act of rebellion against the Dress Act of 1746.

below A 1794 illustration of a Gordon Highlander in his regimental uniform, holding a gun and bayonet.

continue, with some voices strongly supporting the English industrialist story and others disturbed that this theory clashes with a feeling of 'Scottishness' and ignores the practicalities of clothing evolution. Some scholars argue that the kilt simply evolved over time as fashions changed and fabric became more widely available and that the reduction of the garment happened naturally when substantial clothing became unsuitable at the onset of industrial revolution.

The kilt's evolution was also influenced by a regimental tailor in the eighteenth century who neatened its construction with box pleats. Practically this adjustment made the kilt more economical with only 3.2 metres/3½ yards of material in each garment, and gave some Highlanders the opportunity to wear the kilt again. Yet it was really the Victorian upper classes that provided a mass market for the kilt.

THE VICTORIAN KILT

In the early eighteenth century the Highland chiefs took part in the Jacobite risings when the House of Stewart sought to overthrow the Hanoverian monarch. Their final defeat at the Battle of Culloden in 1746 marked a bleak period in Scotland's national pride. The kilt was inevitably associated with the Jacobite rebellion battle garb and the Dress Act under the Act of Proscription was introduced to stifle references to Highland culture.

With the 1746 Act of Proscription came decades of uncertainty in the history of Highland dress. Ordinary Highlanders were forced to adopt lowland suits while the kilt continued to be worn by those excluded from the ban – Lowlanders, Englishmen, Highland regiments and women who were not mentioned in the terms of the Act. Portraiture from the period also suggests that several noblemen rebelled against the ban by commissioning paintings of themselves in full Highland dress. In 1749, a few years after the Proscription Act took effect, John Campbell of Armaddie, the Principal Cashier of the Royal Bank of Scotland, commissioned artist William Mosman to paint his portrait. The picture depicts Campbell boldly wearing a tartan jacket and kilt positioned beside a window overlooking typical Highland countryside, proudly promoting his Scottish ancestry at a time of political unrest.[9]

When the Act was repealed in 1782 by King George III, restrictions on Highland wear were removed and societies were set up with the aim of promoting the kilt once again, but by this time the Highland economy had suffered and couldn't afford to revive the kilt. Essential weaving skills were forgotten, ancient patterns were lost and the kilt almost became obsolete. Fortunately Highland dress was kept alive by both romantic stories and the Highland regiments who increasingly used tartan in their battle garb.

right King George IV holds an audience during a royal visit to Scotland, 1822.

far right Portrait by David Wilkie of King George IV wearing full Scottish dress, 1830.

The fortunes of the *féileadh-beag* subsequently improved in the early 1800s, when there was a revival of tartan, kilts and Highland wear. The Victorians were fanatical about the kilt, desperate to find a family connection to a Highland clan and oblivious to the reality that anyone could wear a kilt regardless of lineage. The kilt was absorbed into the traditional British dress code of the time, which was embraced by Scots who favoured the widely positive connection between the kilt and 'Scottishness'. The Victorians were responsible for categorizing different clan tartans (albeit inaccurately) and devised a double-breasted jacket, 'the doublet', to add further ceremony to the kilt outfit. It had two large tabs at the front separated by a gap for the sporran and four overlapping tabs at the rear. Since then this style has been largely unaltered, and modern Highland dress is 'not a symbol of clan or local associations, but a varietal garb of loud colours and distinctive checks that were mixed and matched to suit the taste of the wearer and which, in certain instances, could be used to symbolize political allegiance.'[10]

King George IV became an inadvertent trendsetter when he wore a kilt during a visit to Edinburgh in 1822. With his nod of approval, the kilt subsequently became a concrete fixture of Scottish identity and heralded a long period of fascination among the Victorian middle classes for all things Highland. Hugh Trevor-Roper said: 'Before 1745, the Highlanders and all their customs were disowned and despised by every articulate Scotchman. After 1845 the Highland takeover was complete. The voice of protest, and of historical truth, was often raised; but it was always powerless. Romanticism might lose its power; but then tourism and commercialism would take over its legacy, extending and vulgarising it in detail.'[11]

Flat or knife pleats became fashionable in the 1860s, and by the 1890s kilts were pleated to their sett rather than their stripe, where each pleat folded in accordance with a particular pattern and mirrored the pattern on the front aprons. This design required up to 8.2 metres/9 yards of fabric and replaced the affordable box-pleat design. So it is clear that the kilt has lived in many different guises, adapting with cultural and political trends and evolving to suit a varying set of demands. Finer details have been modified by generations who have shaped the kilt to suit the needs of their time, but its basic shape has hardly changed since the eighteenth century and its relevance to modern Scotland can't be overlooked.

August 15th 1822.
In Commemoration
of His MAJESTY'S Visit to
SCOTLAND.
A. Afsereti,
G.T. Thatcher,
A. Michie,
Overseers.

MYTHS OF TARTAN

A romantic depiction of Mary Queen of Scots escaping from Lochleven Castle by Craig Shirreff, 1805.

Scotland is often represented as a place of myth and mystery, of hero warriors and romance, as depicted in Sir Walter Scott's stories and poems, in film and in advertising. One of the dominant symbols of the Scottish myth is tartan, which has come to signify nationalism, tradition, rebellion and romance. Figures from Scotland's past are dressed in swathes of tartan, with a bonnet and feather, whether this is historically accurate or not, and a myth of clan tartan was developed by the Victorians. The landscape of Scotland forms part of the mystique, and can resemble a patchwork of plaid with its mottled textures and colours.

The people of the Highlands have often been seen as exotic yet unsophisticated folk with strange customs and superstitions. Dr Johnson, when touring the Highlands in 1773, referred to the people as mysterious as those of 'Borneo and Sumatra',[1] and Scotland as a never-never land has further been reinforced in Hollywood films, in literature and on TV. The Highlands is often represented as a 'sleeping beauty' country, which is forever set in a mythical past but waiting to be awoken. Highland folklore of ghosts and fairies, kelpies and a belief in witches also provided source material for a Scottish myth. We see this in Hollywood musical *Brigadoon*, in ballet *La Sylphide*, the film *Highlander*, Disney animation *Brave* and in TV series *Outlander*, where the Highland way of life is a spell-binding place of the past that can be visited through magic, like Shangri-La or Bali-Hai, and where one can forget all the cares and worries of the modern world.

La Sylphide, believed to be the first romantic ballet when it was performed at the Paris Opera in 1832, helped to reignite a French fascination with the kilt, which had first captivated Parisians following the city's occupation by Highland regiments during the Napoleonic wars. The story tells of a beautiful forest sprite, a witch called Old Madge who lives in a misty forest, and a Scottish farmer – all classic elements of a Scottish fantasy – and the stage costumes for the play used tartan suits and dresses to further reinforce place and time. A twist on the theme was Matthew Bourne's reworking of *La Sylphide* in which he set the ballet in contemporary Glasgow nightclubs.[2]

left A performance of the ballet *La Sylphide* at the theatre of Champs-Elysees, Paris in 1947 with Nina Vyroubova and Roland Petit.

right Siegried Detlev Bendixen's 1854 painting depicts Rob Roy's wife Helen MacGregor as a brave warrior in the conflict at the Pass of Loch Ard.

below right A scene from the television series *Outlander* where tartan is a symbol of entering into a mystical, pre-Culloden Scotland.

below This late 1940s poster for the stage production of *Brigadoon* shows an exaggerated depiction of Scotland's traditional costume.

right Irene Sharaff's costume designs for the 1953 film *Brigadoon* combined modern New Look gowns with touches of tartan.

In fantasy romance *Outlander*, the lead character Claire wears plaid around her shoulders when she finds herself time-travelling from 1945 to 1743, and after being transported into the past she awakens on this piece of fabric, indicating she is now in mythical pre-Culloden Scotland. The 1945 film *I Know Where I'm Going* also features a headstrong Englishwoman who travels to the Hebrides and finds herself stranded during a storm; then the mysticism of Scotland leads her to fall in love with another man and come under a spell within a castle.

BRIGADOON

Vincente Minnelli's *Brigadoon* (1954), starring Gene Kelly, was based on Alan Jay Lerner and Frederick Loewe's successful Broadway musical from 1947. In this, the main character – Tommy Albright – escapes the pressures of New York to visit Scotland on a shooting trip. After getting lost in a misty Scottish glen, he becomes drawn into a fantasy world as he discovers the village of Brigadoon, which awakens only once every 100 years. Irene Sharaff designed the film's costumes, mixing styles from different centuries, including tartan trews, the arisaid, *fèileadh-mòr* and *fèileadh-beag*. The female characters, while supposedly of the eighteenth century, were given a New Look version of Highland dresses, with full skirts, cinched waist and romantic puff sleeves. As part of the publicity for the film, *Brigadoon* dresses were designed and sold in department stores

and advertised in *Vogue*, and in an advert in *Variety* the MGM lion was illustrated wearing Scotch bonnet, kilt, plaid and accessories, doing the Highland fling.[3]

Brigadoon was Hollywood artifice. While Gene Kelly had hoped to film on location in Scotland, it was reported widely that producer Arthur Freed had said that 'Scotland did not look Scottish enough', and so they filmed at the MGM studios instead. Like many films on Scotland, it was 'Hollywood-ified' and the Scottish 'burr' was reduced as producers were concerned that the dialect would be incomprehensible to an American audience.[4]

According to Colin McArthur, *Brigadoon* is 'shorthand for all that is twee and regressive' and was littered with mistakes and stereotypes of Scotland. While the mythologizing of Scottish culture in Scotland is often seen as amusing and comical, in a review on the film's release *The Scotsman* wrote: 'Purple backcloths and excesses of tartan are tolerable on the stage but, seen through the giant eye of CinemaScope, they are ridiculous . . . the director seems to have gone out of his way to make the film as unauthentic as possible. He came to Scotland looking for a filming location and went away disappointed. Scotland was not "Scotch enough".'[5]

The scenery of the film, with its old bridges and glens, inspired the tartanry of American advertising during its 1950s' peak. Whisky such as Old Angus was given the slogan 'A noble Scotch Gentle as a Lamb', and the image of warriors in kilts was used to sell these products.[6]

QUEEN VICTORIA'S FAIRY-TALE KINGDOM

This *Brigadoon* idea of a spellbound land is how Queen Victoria felt on her visits to Balmoral, a place where she could escape from her normal life and where she felt the 'affection of the good people'. She wrote in her Highland diaries of a fete in Deeside in 1859,

Carl Haag's 1854 *Evening at Balmoral, the Stags Brought Home* shows a romantic scene at Balmoral with Queen Victoria being presented with the stags that were hunted during the day by a kilted Prince Albert.

describing 'the Highlanders in their brilliant and picturesque dresses, the wild notes of the pipes, the band, and the beautiful background of mountains, rendered the scene wild and striking in the extreme'.[7]

In 1868 Queen Victoria published her diary of her time in Scotland, under the name *Leaves from the Journal of Our Life in the Highlands*, and she sold a successful 20,000 copies. While Victoria's diaries featured long, flowery prose on the landscapes and weather in Deeside, her writing created a sense of a fairy-tale kingdom, which was captivating to those who read her book. Victoria and Albert, whose design and decor was stamped over the castle, created their own tartan myth with Bavarian spires and Gotha-influenced architecture inspired by Albert's ancestry, and a specially designed Balmoral tartan for interiors and for costume. After Albert's sudden death in 1861, Victoria talked of how she could look only to the past, not to the future, and Balmoral, with its sense of the

'The Highlanders in their brilliant and picturesque dresses, the wild notes of the pipes, the band, and the beautiful background of mountains, rendered the scene wild and striking in the extreme.' Queen Victoria

phantasmagorical, reminded her of happier times with her late husband.[8]

Another aspect of Victoria's Highland fantasy was that she chose to ignore the fact that her Hanoverian ancestors had quelled the 1745 Jacobite rebellion, as well as to overlook the current horror of the Highland Clearances, which were still happening. As historian Antonia Fraser wrote, Victoria 'calmly ignored the fact that the forty-five had been aimed at substituting the Stuart dynasty of Bonnie Prince Charlie for that of the Hanoverians. Instead she was innocently proud of her own Stuart descent (from James I) reserving her frowns for the Tudor Queen Elizabeth I . . .'[9]

Fashion designer Alexander McQueen commented on this with his Highland Rape collection in 1995/1996, by including blood-covered models in MacQueen tartan. As noted by Andrew Bolton in *Anglomania*,[10] McQueen's collection 'intended to counter fanciful and idealistic notions of Scottish history, such as those held by Queen Victoria and her beloved husband.'

MACBETH

One of the early works that depicted Scottish myth and fantasy was William Shakespeare's *Macbeth*, penned around 1605. There have been numerous depictions of it over the years, from paintings to opera, ballet and film, which mostly take a degree of liberty when it comes to creating Scottish costume, particularly Orson Welles' tartan-clad version in 1948. It's believed that Shakespeare wrote the play for James VI (James I of England) who would have been flattered by the play's retelling of the House of Stewart ancestry. Scottish historians of the time believed that the Stewart lineage began with Banquo, whose death was ordered by Macbeth, king of Scots in the mid-eleventh century. Banquo's son escaped to France, where he married and founded the House of Stewart. James VI also believed in witches and mysticism, and claimed to have come across three witches in North Berwick, who created a storm in the North Sea.[11]

BRAVEHEART'S HISTORICAL RE-IMAGININGS

The popularity of films such as *Braveheart* and *Rob Roy* in the 1990s reconstructed the dress of the Highlanders to create a sense of macho ruggedness. The rebellious plaid of *Braveheart* linked into the trend for grunge fashion that was happening around the same time as the film's release. After *Braveheart* it became more common to see this belted plaid look at Highland gatherings, as opposed to the formal dress kilt. However, there is no evidence that belted plaid was worn before the sixteenth century, and so for a film set in 1280 it was inaccurate. As historian Sharon L. Krossa documented: 'In the thirteenth century (and the fourteenth, fifteenth and most of the sixteenth), no Scots, whether Gaels or not, wore belted plaids (let alone kilts of any kind).

left One of several 'harlequin' portraits of Bonnie Prince Charlie dating from the eighteenth century, with the prince in a fancifully coloured check suit.

above A mythical tartan-swathed hero prince says farewell to Flora MacDonald in this 1905 print that appeared in Cassell's *History of England* volume 4.

Further, when the Scottish Gaels did start wearing their belts outside their plaids (mantles), they did not wear them in the rather bizarre style depicted in the film.'[12]

Mel Gibson, when interviewed in 2009, described how artistic licence was taken to construct a folk hero from limited information available at the time. 'He wasn't as nice as the character we saw up there on the screen', Gibson said of William Wallace. 'We romanticized him a bit. We shifted the balance because someone's got to be the good guy against the bad guy; that's the way stories are told.'[13]

Braveheart is a fantasy version of William Wallace, distorting the time frames and locations in Scotland in order to create a narrative. Although the costumes may not be historically accurate, audiences expect to see the Scottish characters wearing tartan in a film about medieval Scotland. While critics were keen to point out the factual inaccuracies, the film ignited a sense of passion within Scotland, resulting in Wallace's adoption as a representative for Scottish independence, and a statue of Wallace was raised in Stirling, which was not dissimilar to Mel Gibson's appearance in the film.

BONNIE PRINCE CHARLIE

Hollywood was not the only place to produce a romanticized version of Scotland. Following the Act of Union in 1707 tartan became a popular way to express anti-union sentiment and loyalty to the Stuart crown. Portraits of Jacobite figures in the seventeenth century depicted them in tartan and with a white rose, cockade or ribbon to indicate their allegiance to the Jacobite cause. Following the Jacobite defeat at Culloden, and the enforcement of the Act of Proscription 1746, a tartan myth was created around Bonnie Prince Charlie, in which fragments of tartan claimed to have been worn by the prince were passed down over the years. At the National Museum of Scotland there are a number of tartan fragments allegedly worn by him, but which when tested were found to have been machine woven in the 1820s. This was a period of romantic interest in Jacobite relics following George IV's visit. At the Culloden Battlefield Visitor's Centre, there is a blanket of tartan woven in 1996 by James Pringle Weavers. It was reconstructed from a fragment of plaid believed to have been worn by Bonnie Prince Charlie, after he sought refuge on Arisaig and was given a suit to wear by Lady Catriona MacDonald.

Portraits of Bonnie Prince Charlie dating from around the Battle of Culloden created an image of a Scottish prince dressed in tartan. However, often these works were drawn from earlier paintings, with tartan detail added in, or were of his brother Henry, further distancing his image from reality. A 1750 painting by William Mosman of Prince Charles Edward Stuart (to give him his official title) was based on an earlier portrait by Louis Gabriel Blanchet of the young prince dressed in armour. Mosman kept the young,

clockwise from top left Flora MacDonald, painted by Richard Wilson in 1747, wearing the red tartan and white ribbons that signified she was a Jacobite; Katharine Hepburn in *Mary of Scotland* (1936), an extravagant Hollywood depiction of the queen; Cara Delevingne at Chanel's 2012 Métiers d'Art show at Linlithgow Palace, the birthplace of Mary Queen of Scots.

boyish face, but instead dressed the prince in a tartan jacket and plaid and with a cockade in his hat. Lucinda Lax from the Scottish National Portrait Gallery in Edinburgh said: 'In the early portraits Charles is very much the European court prince, wearing French fashions, the garter sash, but there's a shift around 1746 where his image changes to wearing tartan. However, one interesting portrait by Allan Ramsay, believed to have been from a sitting in 1745, shows Charles in European dress.' This 'lost' portrait of Charlie was recently discovered, and is the only known portrait of Bonnie Prince Charlie that was painted while he was in Scotland. The twenty-four year old sat for the portrait in Holyrood Palace in October 1745, and is wearing the costume of a European prince.[14]

After his defeat at Culloden, Charles was pursued by government forces across the Highlands and Hebrides during the summer of 1746. The £30,000 price on his head attracted huge interest and excitement over where the prince could be and if he would be caught. A wanted poster from the time depicted Bonnie Prince Charlie dressed in a tartan suit – a comical idea that he could be identified by a fantasy costume and construct of his image. Similarly, the 'harlequin' portraits, from around 1750, of which there are at least twenty, depicted Bonnie Prince Charlie in fanciful Highland costume with a backdrop of castle and mountains. The checked fabric is similar to that worn by Italian harlequins, hence the name.[15]

JACOBITE WOMEN

Mary Queen of Scots is another of Scotland's figures where myth crosses into fact. There is no evidence that she wore tartan, particularly as she was a French Catholic woman who was more likely to have adopted crucifixes and fashionable ruffs. However, when Chanel in 2012 re-imagined the court of Mary Queen of Scots for the annual Métier d'Arts show at Linlithgow Palace, lace collars were combined with tartan scarves, woollen coats and Scotch bonnets for a fantasy depiction of the Stewarts. Similarly, Katharine Hepburn in *Mary of Scotland* played the queen in lace collars and Renaissance gowns, but wore plaid across her shoulders and a huge feather in her bonnet – a fabled Jacobite warrior version of Mary Queen of Scots. In the eighteenth century Jacobite women held a fascination among the public, particularly rebel heroines whose crossing of gender stereotypes was bold and exciting. Miss Jenny Cameron was labelled 'Jenny the bold Amazon of the north' after it was said she led 250 men to join Bonnie Prince Charlie at Glenfinnan. There is an etching from around 1753 that depicts her as a warrior figure in tartan trews and jacket.[16]

One of the most recognizable images of Flora MacDonald is a painting from 1747 by Richard Wilson. It was painted for a young naval officer on the ship that took her to London after helping Bonnie Prince Charlie escape. Despite being held in the Tower of London for a short time, she became a cause célèbre

in London. In the painting she wears a red tartan dress with white ribbons to identify her as a Jacobite.[17]

MYTH-MAKING IN THE NINETEENTH CENTURY

Sir Walter Scott was perhaps most influential in setting the mood for romantic Scotland with the publication of his first poem 'Lady in the Lake' in 1810 and his Waverley novels, which captured the romance of the '45 rebellion. Loch Katrine, which featured in Scott's 'Lady in the Lake', attracted tourists who could take a boat to Ellen's Isle, named after the heroine. Scott's stories were frequently turned into theatre productions in the nineteenth century because, in the absence of copyright, his works could be adapted and used in performance. Tartan would often be combined with armour for the stage costumes, to reinforce the brave Scottish warrior and offer a romantic escapism from industrialization.

With the popularity of Scott's works, Scotland became a fashionable tourist destination, and visitors wished to absorb the culture by wearing tartan, much like the fashion for orientalism in the late nineteenth century. As Antonia Fraser said: 'Scott's works turned the public imagination northwards in a way for which it is difficult to find a parallel, except perhaps in the rise of chinoiserie when European travellers rediscovered the Far East.'[18]

Because of this fascination with Scottish tradition, people really wanted to believe in the ancient stories of the clans and their tartan, which is why they fell for myth-makers such as the Sobieski Stuarts as well as for James Macpherson's hugely popular Ossian poems,

left Loch Katrine became a popular Victorian tourist attraction as the setting for Ellen's Isle in Sir Walter Scott's *The Lady of the Lake*, as shown in this painting by John Knox in 1815.

below An 1867 engraving by Thomas Brown showing Scott's heroine Ellen in *The Lady of the Lake*, wrapped in a large piece of plaid.

supposedly translated from ancient Gaelic material. However, the myth around a fantasy version of Scottish history was acknowledged even back in 1871. It was reported in a *New York Times* piece that 'Scott invented the modern Highlander. It is to him more than to anybody else that we owe the strange perversion that induces a good Lowland Scot to fancy himself more nearly allied to the semi-barbarous wearers of the tartan than to his blood relations.'[19]

Scottish myth and romance continue to hold fascination, as the symbols of Scotland take on a mystical meaning through literature, fashion and film. Marc Jacobs' autumn/winter 2004/2005 collection for Louis Vuitton used tartan with glamour, mixing goth and punk. He called it a 'Tim Burton view of the Highlands', using glamorous touches from the 1930s and 1940s.[20]

In Disney's *Brave*, a fiery Scottish princess with flame-red hair finds herself caught up in magic after visiting a witch in a forest lair. Disney designed its own tartan for the film for three fictional clans, and a red tartan that was similar to the real clan Mackintosh; these were registered through the Scottish Register of Tartans. Visit Scotland championed the film as a strong advert for Scotland, noting that 'the film is a fantastic showcase for Scotland with Merida's adventures bringing to life much of the inspiration that attracts visitors to our shores.'[21] Just like the romantic view of Scotland in the nineteenth century, the myth of Scotland was treated as if part of reality.

I LUV
BAY CITY

THE POPULARITY OF TARTAN

Bay City Rollers fans prove their allegiance to the band with tartan scarves and trimmings.

Tartan is a lot more than misty glens, bagpipes, haggis and shortbread – it can be rebellious, masculine and cool. Its colours can be loud or harmonious, autumnal or vivid. It's a fabric for musicians, pop stars and coquettes, for fashionable 1950s' New Yorkers or Shoreditch hipsters, and it has transcended its origins as a fabric of the Highlands to reach out around the world. Tartan has gone through many evolutions, from practical woven fabric for protecting against the harsh elements of the Highlands, to a symbol of rebellious uprising after the Battle of Culloden. It would be reasonable to say it's the most politicized of cloths – there's no other fabric that acts as such a nationalistic symbol for a particular country while also evoking countless meanings and interpretations.

Following its ban after Culloden, tartan lost its original purpose as a versatile cloth for the harsh Scottish outdoors. Instead it became the uniform of Highland regiments; it was worn at balls and clubs dedicated to preserving Scottish history and romanticizing the notion of the Highlander; and it took on a life of its own as a fashionable fabric for men and women.

Following the union of the Scottish and English throne in 1603 and then the Act of Union 1707, waves of forced and voluntary migration took place across Scotland. One result of this was that tartan spread across the world, particularly enabling migrants to hold on to their roots while establishing a new home. As Richard Blaustein wrote in his book *The Thistle and the Brier*: 'a new global Scottish culture was coming into being, and nostalgic immigrants were playing a key role in its creation.'[1]

Over the last hundred years tartan has transformed from old-fashioned and twee, as a decoration on shortbread tins, to a symbol of many different street-style movements – punk, grunge and skater. This in turn has inspired high-end fashion, from Vivienne Westwood to Jean Paul Gaultier. Tartan is the uniform of lumberjacks and country-and-western singers, it's worn by schoolgirls, fetishized in Japanese manga and pop music videos, and is the loud performance piece of glam rock. Tartan has a do-it-yourself feel to it, as pieces of tartan can be used to create a new look and style. It can be ripped up into strips, tied around the waist or worn over T-shirts, while plaid skirts are adapted into micro-minis. It's here that tartan achieves polarity – when women wear tartan it is feminine, and on men it demonstrates a form of rugged masculinity. Maybe part of the reason behind tartan's eternal popularity is that it's a fabric for both the Establishment and the rebel. The Stewart tartan was adopted by punks in the 1970s due to its links as the official tartan of Elizabeth II as well as to the Jacobites as they fought to reinstate a Stewart king on the throne of Britain.

Because different tartans are categorized and assigned to particular clans, with an infinite variety of setts, it is a useful fabric for uniforms and can demonstrate an

above *Vogue* magazine cover from October 1924 of a woman in a fashionable plaid hunting outfit.

right Harry Lauder was often seen as a Scottish caricature, as shown with this artwork for the sheet music of *Early in the Morning* from 1908.

allegiance to a gang or a group. This is why those with Scottish heritage are keen to discover what the tartan for their surname is. It creates a sense of belonging and an understanding of their perceived history. Tartan is also a comforting fabric that evokes fond memories with its connection to country music and old-fashioned Americana. Taylor Swift, in one song, remembers the 'plaid shirt days' of a lost love, and it's been said that tartan sales surged in the months after 9/11 in New York.[2]

In the last decade tartan has gained immense popularity as a reaction to the metrosexual look of high-powered financiers, as represented by bands such as Mumford and Sons and Bon Iver. The hipster style of tartan shirt, skinny jeans and beard became de rigueur, with a return to folksy music and grungy rawness. With a generation of young people experiencing uncertain times, living through economic recession and political instability, the checked shirt has become a wardrobe essential once again.

THE TARTAN ARMY

Worn by clansmen in battle, tartan still evokes the warrior spirit and has become the patriotic fabric for the Tartan Army, descending en masse to support the Scottish football team. They appropriate the classic Highland dress of kilt and sporran, but often combined with football shirts, work boots and an exaggerated tam o' shanter or Jimmy hat. Their uniform mimics traditional Highland clothing but with a modern twist that reflects football 'casual' trends. This Tartan Army look was reinvigorated in the mid-1990s by Scottish-themed films, particularly

left The checked shirt has shifted from blue collar shirt to a component of street style and hipster fashion.

above A model wearing the Braveheart-style plaid and blue paint at the Dressed to Kilt show at New York's Tartan Week in 2006.

right Vivienne Westwood's punky update of the kilt at the 2006 Edinburgh International Fashion Festival.

Braveheart and *Rob Roy*. Both these films apparently depicted the raw, original way of wearing a kilt, with the plaid thrown over one shoulder. Along with this traditional, 'honest' way of wearing tartan, blue-painted faces, believed to have been a warrior sign of the Picts using woad, became popular at football games because of the influence of *Braveheart*.

While there are many jokes in popular culture about a kilt being akin to a man wearing a skirt, there's also the common saying that nothing is worn under a kilt, which adds to the ruggedness and bravado of the wearer. The Scotsman in his kilt is hardy enough not to require protection from the elements, and risqué enough to flash himself if he takes to it. French cartoons dating from when Highland regiments occupied Paris in 1815 satirized women's curiosity over what was worn underneath their kilts.[3] This joke was also played out in *Braveheart*, when the men in Wallace's army lift up their kilts and moon the English opposition. The rugged man in a kilt has become a sexual fantasy played with humour, as seen in a popular advert for Scott's porridge oats. Rory

McCann is the alpha male in white vest and kilt, but with an underlying comic value as he emerges from an ice cold loch with only a sporran to cover his modesty. In 1998 Ewan McGregor was photographed for *Vanity Fair* magazine by Annie Leibovitz in a Stewart tartan kilt, rough shirt and waistcoat and holding a rooster, which reinforced the 'sexy charm' of the kilted Scot.[4]

SCOTS MIGRATION TO NORTH AMERICA

The eighteenth century saw large-scale Scottish migration to North America with colonies established from the east coast to the southern states of the US. As they travelled along the Great Wagon Road from Pennsylvania, it's likely that the Scots brought tartan with them. In 1736 a colony of Highlanders in Georgia was established, and the trustees ordered 274 metres/300 yards of tartan from Inverness to provide for soldiers protecting the land from the Spanish.[5]

By the 1770s, some 50,000 Scottish settlers had arrived in North Carolina. Some like Flora MacDonald were Jacobite supporters fleeing after Culloden, while others had been deported to the colonies as punishment for other crimes. A second wave of migration took place from the 1820s following a cholera outbreak, a famine and forced eviction of crofters under the Highland Clearances. Highland regiments were also sent to the New World, and in 1758 the 42nd Royal Highland Regiment of Foot, or the Black Watch, fought during the French and Indian wars, dressed in the regimental Black Watch kilt and with the wail of the pipes heard as a battle cry.[6]

Tartan has become associated with the hillbilly, a group of people traditionally from the Appalachia,

left Catherine Bach's knotted plaid shirt and tiny denim cut-offs as worn in *The Dukes of Hazzard* sparked an early 1980s trend.

above Ranchers in their plaid work shirts branding cattle in Keogh, North Dakota in the 1960s.

the mountain range that cuts a ridge through the east coast and into the southern states of the US. It is known for its Scottish and Scots–Irish heritage, with rich traditions of plaid, fiddle music and moonshine. Whisky-making and drinking were traditions that went back to Scotland and Ulster, where lowland Scots had settled under King James VI. Mountain living was wild and rough, and the hillbillies set themselves apart from the rest of America with a clan-like social structure.

In the 1920s this stereotype would see the hillbilly character represented in George Hay's *Grand Ole Opry*, comic *Lil' Abney* and TV series *The Beverley Hillbillies*, dressed with overalls and plaid shirts, taking on a rough, uncultured meaning. In 1979 TV series *The Dukes of Hazzard* was first aired, and the hillbilly plaid shirt was given a sexy makeover as Daisy Duke teamed hers with a pair of hot pants. A huge trend was launched for tying the shirt around the waist, to reveal a preferably toned and tanned stomach.

For those in other areas of North America influenced by Scottish migration, there is a fascination and celebration of the 'tartanry' of Scottish culture. Nova Scotia in Canada still has strong connections to Scotland, with a special tartan as an emblem and a Scottish cultural influence of fiddles and ceilidh. The Grandfather Mountain Highland

left Dolly Parton in 1984 wearing the uniform of country and western singers – a plaid shirt and cowboy hat.

above Marlon Brando's buffalo plaid jacket in *On the Waterfront* (1954) indicated his rebellious, blue collar credentials.

right The Beach Boys in their favoured Pendleton shirts during a photo shoot for the cover of *Surfer Girl*.

Games in North Carolina can attract up to 40,000 people, with many dressed in kilts. 'It is personal identification with the specific combination of kilt and tartan that is significant for Scottish-American identity expression,' said Ian Maitland Hume in *From Tartan to Tartanry*.[7]

THE BLUE COLLAR SHIRT

Scots immigration to the southern states and Canada would influence the ubiquity of the plaid shirt, worn by lumberjacks and blue-collar workers, and cementing it as one of the most masculine of fabrics – raw, basic, casual and rugged. The plaid shirt has become the ultimate symbol of comfort, entrenched in both subcultures and the mainstream. As well as representing masculinity, it has the homespun craft element, with tartan and plaid home furnishings creating an 'at home on the prairie' feel. Country music in the southern states of America can be traced to the Scottish folk songs and fiddle music that had travelled on a migrant's journey, along with Presbyterian hymns that would form a basis for gospel music.[8] Scottish heritage was combined with the lonesome cowboy to form the style of the country-and-western singer – a checked shirt, cowboy boots and Stetson hat.

John Fogerty of Creedence Clearwater Revival became known for his trademark checked shirt, which played up to the idea of the working man, through folk and country music traditions. He once commented

that he was 'proud of' being known as 'the father of the flannel shirt'.[9] He told the *Toronto Sun* in 2014: 'People look at my closet and find nine of the same plaid shirt. I love flannel plaid shirts and cowboy shirts, western shirts. I'm certainly a connoisseur.'[10]

In the nineteenth century the tartan shirt became popular with farmworkers and cattle herders for its durability. In 1850 Pennsylvania clothing company Woolrich launched a plaid flannel Buffalo Check shirt in the two-tone, red-and-black Rob Roy check. It was created by a designer who owned a herd of buffalo, and it would become a bestseller among outdoor workers.[11]

This red-and-black Buffalo Check would come to represent lumberjack folk hero Paul Bunyan when the Red River Lumber Company featured his image in its advertising in 1914. Bunyan was depicted in cartoons,

'Plaid seems to have caught the fancy of designers for early autumn. Large and small, in woollens and taffetas, for daytime and evening, they claim attention.' *New York Times*, July 1949

statues and on woodland trail signs as a symbol of ideal 'outdoor' masculinity, just like the Scot in his kilt.

The wool shirt was warm, durable and offered excellent protection against the elements, but typically the colour choice had been limited. Pendleton, an American clothing company, developed the plaid further when it created its bestselling working man's wool shirt in 1924 in a variety of colours and using their unique Oregon Umatilla wool. This was 'something better than other mills can or will make', as owner Charles Pleasant Bishop wrote. Pendleton was inspired by its colourful 'Indian trade' blankets, and took from them the idea to develop vivid shirts. These colourful wool shirts were immediately popular, and by the 1950s they became a staple in male wardrobes, reflecting the post-war concept of leisure time.[12]

After the Second World War, and with GIs (US soldiers) given funding to go to university, society became increasingly democratized.[13] The result was a casual adoption of plaid shirts and jeans in everyday wear. Plaid shirts harked back to the cowboy to represent honest, hardworking American values. In *On the Waterfront* (1954) Marlon Brando wore a red tartan work jacket throughout the film, demonstrating his position as a blue-collar worker. Brando, like Jack Kerouac and James Dean, represented a new type of masculinity, both troubled and rebellious, and, following the beat generation's concept of 'downward mobility', they dressed in jeans and plaid. Compared to the standard male dress of suit and tie, Kerouac stood out in a Buffalo Check shirt, and the overwhelming popularity of the beatniks by the late 1950s inspired a complete relaxation of dress over the following decades.

Plaid, along with check Madras fabric, was used for swimming trunks, golf trousers and jackets and in particular the Pendleton shirt became the must-have item for surfers, worn over board shorts or with Levi's. The Beach Boys, originally named the Pendletones, reinforced the shirt's popularity when they were photographed for the cover of *Surfer Girl* in their checked shirts while lined up holding a surfboard.

TARTAN IN TWENTIETH-CENTURY WOMEN'S FASHION

The 1920s saw a revolution in women's clothing as skirts were shortened to an unprecedented knee-length, and pyjama trousers became a daring fashion. Tartan was incorporated into clothing as a twist on traditional male items of clothes. With more women taking up sports in the 1920s for leisure and as a way of keeping fashionably trim, tartan came to be used in new sports clothes, just as it had been with men's fashion. Forward-thinking couturier Paul Poiret, who had invented the lampshade tunic and harem pants, created short silk dresses using a bright pattern in coral, grey, white and black, which were both girlish and fresh in their use of check.[14]

right A Paul Poiret silk taffeta day dress in pink, black and grey tartan from the mid-1920s, part of the V&A collection.

following pages Models displaying tartan fashions in New York from a photoshoot in *Vogue* in 1958.

below Ginger Rogers and Fred Astaire do a vaudevillian Highland number in the 1949 *The Barkleys of Broadway*.

right Ali MacGraw in *Love Story* (1970) set a trend for the classic preppy look of tartan scarves and plaid skirts.

bottom right The Windmill Girls perform in risqué Highland costume at the Windmill Theatre, London in 1940.

As women came into the workplace in the 1930s and 1940s, tartan was popular for smart suits and dresses. In July 1949, The *New York Times* reported on the big new trend for plaid: 'Plaid seems to have caught the fancy of designers for early autumn. Large and small, in woollens and taffetas, for daytime and evening, they claim attention. Names familiar in the history of clans are frequently heard when sporty costumes are presented. Less conventional are plaids in modern design, bringing new colour combinations into being. Plaids will flock to college campuses, they'll enter the sedate atmosphere of business offices and the gay glamour of city restaurants, and they'll travel abroad.'[15]

By the early 1950s, plaid was found across a huge range of clothing for women, from check shirts, scarves and berets, to extravagant New Look gowns. By the 1970s, after several years of boho chic, tartan came into fashion again as Ivy League style was embraced once more. Ali MacGraw's look in the 1970 film *Love Story* heralded the re-emergence of a preppy style, with plaid skirts and tartan scarves, warm knits and hats.

TARTAN FOR SATURDAY NIGHT ENTERTAINMENT

In the late nineteenth century tartan became a popular fabric for music-hall performers, for its comic, twee connotations and as a cosy symbol of Scottish dress on the light entertainment scene. Sir Harry Lauder was a vaudeville singer who achieved international acclaim with his romanticized Scottish songs such as 'I Love a Lassie'. By 1911 he was the most popular international singer, touring the world in Highland dress and attracting an audience of migrant Scots who missed their homeland.

Noddy Holder, Slade's frontman, was famous for his loud tartan suits with cut-off trousers – an influence for the Bay City Rollers style.

Because performers such as Lauder, Jock Mills and Jack Lorimer had only a short time on stage to impress, their tartan costumes were exaggerated in order to stand out. As Dr Paul Maloney wrote, their costumes with the loud checks, bonnets and sporran had to present 'a version of Highland dress deliberately scaled up to be seen'.[16] When Harry Lauder arrived in New York in 1907 in full Highland dress, queues stretched around the block, and his type of vaudeville would be an inspiration for Broadway and Hollywood, where imagery was vital for creating interesting musical performances. Stan Laurel and Oliver Hardy starred in *Bonnie Scotland* in 1935; in *The Barkleys of Broadway*, Fred Astaire and Ginger Rogers danced a Lauder-inspired Highland fling; while *Brigadoon* used twee Scottish imagery in the Broadway show and MGM musical.[17]

Scottish music-hall characters Andy Stewart and Jimmy Shand wore their patriotic Highland regalia on the TV show *White Heather Club*, from 1957 to 1968, which also aired as a Hogmanay special. The *White Heather Club* reinforced the 'tartan and shortbread' view of Scotland with kilts and folk music, and ladies in white dresses and tartan sashes. Andy Stewart's most famous song 'Donald Where's Your Troosers?' was about the reaction in London to a Scot in a kilt, including an ironic Elvis impersonation, while hit song 'A Scottish Soldier' was pure Scottish sentimentality. At the same time as Andy Stewart was doing his act on *Scotch Corner* in the 1970s, rock musicians and the punk scene were adopting tartan as a performance piece but using it to create a very different meaning.

GLAM ROCK

In the early 1970s, bohemian fashion turned to glam rock, with stars such as Marc Bolan and Rod Stewart choosing big hair, glittering jackets and huge, exaggerated platform shoes. For these artists costume was performance, and tartan – with its links to vaudeville – created a sense of camp theatricality. English band Slade had originally been skinheads, but

Rod Stewart, pictured in the 1970s, used tartan as a performance piece that paid tribute to his Scottish roots.

they transformed into glam rock, with Noddy Holder decked out in tartan suits and his trademark mirror top hat worn over his long hair. Meanwhile in the US, the New York Dolls also picked up on tartan in their stage outfits that blurred gender lines.

Rod Stewart, despite growing up in Essex, wore Royal Stewart tartan proudly in tribute to his Edinburgh-born father and his claimed connections to Stirling Castle, home of the Stewarts. During his idol days he had a habit of going bare-chested except for a tartan scarf around his neck, or else of performing in a tartan shirt, football scarf and shiny skin-tight trousers on the *Kenny Everett Show*, his hair always done up in Modish spikes. Rod Stewart also added touches of tartan to shimmering suits or leopard-skin outfits bought from the rock star shop of choice, Granny Takes a Trip boutique on the King's Road. Granny's was where Mick Jagger purchased his tartan velvet jacket, worn on the inside cover of the Rolling Stone's *Exile on Main Street*.

In a 1973 interview with magazine *Sounds*, the journalist noted of Rod Stewart: 'I am transfixed by a black and white tartan wool scarf draped round his neck. It is held together by an authentic Scotch brooch . . . At this point I would like you to remember that the temperature is rising ten degrees a second. It is, should it be needed, conclusive proof that Mr Stewart's fierce nationalistic pride is beginning to reach masochistic proportions.'[18]

The Bay City Rollers, a group of young Edinburgh heart-throbs, briefly sparked 'tartanmania' across the world from 1975. Looking back on their outfits, with their tartan-trimmed culottes and scarves held aloft, it's hard to believe they were setting trends, but it was easy for teenagers to replicate. All they needed was to add a tartan trim to trousers, or tie a scarf around the neck as a pledge of allegiance to the Rollers.[19] A reporter from *The Times*, who was in Australia in 1975 when the Bay City Rollers toured, remarked that 'everywhere I go in Australia I am mobbed by shrieking teenage girls, all wearing tartan favours'.[20] It was complete fan loyalty verging on hysteria, where tartan demonstrated allegiance and devotion. As Chris Brown wrote in *Booted and Suited*, his account of 1970s' hooligan fashion, the Bay City Rollers took the fashions started by Rod Stewart and Slade to the extreme, with their army of fans in baggy culottes with tartan piping: 'Bright red braces, tartan scarves and rainbow-coloured socks completed the fashion disaster, which was in truth a parody of the skinhead gear of a few years earlier.'[21]

PUNK

While tartan transitioned from music-hall performance to a glam-rock fashion statement, it was the punk movement that fully revived it as a symbol of rebellion. The red-and-black Royal Stewart tartan was the preferred punk fabric, as it stood for both support of,

Los Angeles punks in 1984 creating their own look by adapting tartan kilts and trousers.

and rebellion against, the Establishment. The Royal Stewart tartan is the official tartan of Queen Elizabeth II, and it was also the tartan of the House of Stewart, worn by Bonnie Prince Charlie and the Jacobites. Traditionally it has been said that people can wear the Royal Stewart tartan only if they have express permission of the queen, so for punks to wear it reflected their anarchist spirit in mocking the aristocracy. They wore strips of Royal Stewart fabric with leather, safety pins and distressed denim, to create a unique DIY, deconstructed style. There was a further twist on the use of the Royal Stewart tartan when the Sex Pistols released *God Save the Queen*. The anthem, first sung in 1745 in support of George II, with the line 'the rebellious Scots to crush', was now treated with irony and contempt.

Vivienne Westwood and Malcolm McLaren are considered the founders of the punk movement in Britain, with their boutique on the King's Road

right Madonna in Jean Paul Gaultier cyber-punk stage costumes for her Drowned World tour in 2001.

bottom right Rihanna during the filming of the video for *We Found Love* in 2011, a song produced by Scottish DJ Calvin Harris.

where they sold controversial slogan T-shirts, adapted rock 'n' roll memorabilia and reconstructed Teddy-boy suits. It was in 1976, when McLaren and Westwood's shop was renamed Sedentaries, that tartan was first used in their collections. Westwood created a tartan bondage suit with parachute straps, which combined fetishism and politics with the Second World War imagery she was also referencing at the time.[22] For former Sex Pistol John Lydon, his use of tartan was also partly inspired by childhood: 'I've loved tartan all my life, but that's the way my mum and dad used to dress me as a child. It was always little plaid suits with shorts and little tartan waistcoats.'[23]

Not only would tartan be used again and again by Vivienne Westwood in her collections, but other fashion designers would be inspired by this subversive use of a traditional fabric. Alexander McQueen chose the MacQueen tartan for his Highland Rape collection in London in 1995, mixing tartan with violent, rebellious imagery that told the story of the Highland Clearances.

Jean Paul Gaultier was inspired by punk's use of tartan for his later designs. 'I saw the punks wear it when I started going to London in the 1970s', he commented. 'That's where I understood that (tartan) could be subversive. I embraced it and keep coming back to it. It's a traditional fabric, used throughout the centuries, which suddenly became a symbol of rebellion and anti-conformism.'[24]

When Gaultier created costumes for Madonna's Drowned World tour in 2001, he used a concept of a cyberpunk with Scottish influence. The tartan kilt worn over bondage trousers and with a mesh zip-top not only played up to this reinvented punk imagery, but also referenced Madonna's love affair with Scotland at that time. In December 2000 she married Guy Ritchie at Skibo Castle, Sutherland, with Ritchie in a kilt in the Hunting Mackintosh tartan, Madonna in a Stella McCartney dress with tartan detail, and a ceilidh for entertainment after a haggis dinner. She was quoted as saying: 'Scotland is dripping in atmosphere. It is so beautiful . . . you know, ultimately I'm a romantic. And my husband and I are both obsessed with history, and we wanted to go to a place that had history. He has really helped me appreciate the rawness and roughness of nature.'[25]

Madonna made it very fashionable for celebrities to hold their own Scottish wedding, as *The Guardian* newspaper wrote in December 2000, in an article entitled 'Brigadoon is alive with the sound of money'. It said: 'Tourism is the Highlands' lifeblood and has been in decline. But within days of the wedding announcement, tourist offices were inundated with requests for information. A website to promote Highland weddings received 6,000 hits in its first week. It is estimated that Madonna's event could bring £1.5 million to the local economy in the next few weeks.'[26]

Tartan carries on the glam-rock and punk ethos as a rebellious stage uniform for pop stars, or by creating a girlish innocence with tartan dresses. With its connection to vaudeville and American folk music, tartan is often seen as a fabric for camp stage costume – the wearer of a tartan suit grabs attention with its vibrant colours, just as Highlanders wore the fabric to demonstrate their sense of fashion with the brightest hues. Pop stars such as Rihanna, Taylor Swift and Paloma Faith have also chosen strong tartan suits as statement pieces, while Gwen Stefani wore tartan skateboarder trousers with a midriff-revealing top, which reflected her punk and ska roots.

GRUNGE FASHION

While fashions in the 1980s represented the Reagan and Thatcher era of yuppies, power-dressing and Wall Street financiers in pin-stripes, braces and expensive watches, the 1990s shifted tack with the grunge movement. It was a style that was easy to wear; you could pick a check shirt from a charity shop or cheap clothing store and throw it on over a T-shirt. As grunge had emerged from the Washington punk scene, plaid was worn in the same DIY way as the punks of the 1970s, but with a skateboarder influence of practical flannel shirts and ripped jeans. Grunge was more wearable and less conspicuous than punk as you could blend into the background with a tartan shirt tied around the waist or layered over a

T-shirt, and the plaid shirt demonstrated solid, grounded values as a working man's uniform. Ironically grunge, like punk, soon swept into haute couture, with Marc Jacobs designing a grunge collection for Perry Ellis in 1993, which was heavily criticized at the time for creating a designer look from what was ultimately an anti-fashion movement.[27]

THE SCHOOLGIRL LOOK

As education was provided for more children during the nineteenth century, tartan was used to create school uniforms that were based on adult outfits, and this Victorian legacy is still evident with the school kilts in modern schoolgirl uniforms. In America, while high schools generally have no uniform, Catholic schools enforce a uniform policy of plaid skirt, jumper and blouse. Tartan works particularly well for school skirts as it can be designed to follow the school's official colours and ethos, attributing a sense of belonging to everyone who wears that sett. While the homogenous nature of the school uniform removes a sense of individuality, schoolgirls often customize and adapt the way they wear their uniform in order to assert their identity and by shortening their skirts to show that they are grown up and independent.

As more and more women went to work and to college, tartan became a preppy uniform for college campuses, as smart office wear and for wealthy Manhattanites. In *Breathless: An American Girl in Paris*, Nancy Miller described the look of New York's Upper East Side in the 1960s: 'blue blazer and Gucci loafers (also blue), Black Watch plaid, pleated skirt . . .'[28]

Fashions in the 1960s incorporated more girlish touches to women's clothing, which were an antithesis to the structured, sophisticated 'New Look' dress of the 1950s. Tartan A-line dresses and skirts worn with Mary Jane shoes and long socks reflected tartan's use in children's clothing and the school uniform, but, when worn by Anna Karina in Jean Luc Godard's *Band of Outsiders*, with a black jumper, it was coquettish yet chic. In the 1970s tartan acted as a counter to the hippie, bohemian fashions, which had been the dominant look of the late 1960s.

In Japan, the school uniform was representative of the *sukeban* (bad girl), as seen in the film *Sailor Suit and Machine Gun*, and the TV series *Terrifying Girls' High School*, where schoolgirls demonstrated violent tendencies in their sailor-suit uniforms. After the Japanese

below *Twin Peak*'s Audrey Horne was often seen in pleated tartan skirt and sweater, as an innocent 1950s-style *femme fatale*.

right Anna Karina in Jean-Luc Godard's *Band of Outsiders* (1964) – a beatnik coquette in tartan skirt and black sweater.

Clueless (1995) turned grunge fashion on its head with a cool adaptation of the schoolgirl uniform.

In Quentin Tarantino's *Kill Bill Volume 1*, Chiaki Kuriyama plays a schoolgirl assassin, influenced by the bad girl in a school uniform in Japanese Manga.

school uniform was changed to a pleated skirt, the image of the *sukeban* in Manga was adapted to depict girls in tartan skirts.[29] Quentin Tarantino would reference this in *Kill Bill* with a psychotic assassin schoolgirl in a school blazer and tartan skirt, brandishing a spiked ball and chain, as the tartan skirt, with the innocent, uniform qualities, was subverted. It was influenced by a 1990s cult of girls in Japan, known as *kogals*, who wore their school uniforms in a sexualized way, with shortened tartan or plain pleated skirts, baggy socks, weejun loafers and their sweaters tied around their waists.From the Japanese kogal subculture, to Britney Spears and the film *Clueless*, the 1990s experienced a socially acceptable mainstream fashion for fetishizing the schoolgirl uniform, where the kilt became hyper-sexualized. The pleated tartan skirts and sweaters worn by Audrey Horne in *Twin Peaks* helped to convey her character as a schoolgirl femme fatale. Liv Tyler in *Empire Records* and with Alicia Silverstone in Aerosmith's *Crazy* video made tartan skirts cool and slightly dangerous, while late 1990s' high-school films such as *The Craft* also followed the fashion for plaid skirts.

Clueless was the hit teen film of 1995, heralding a move away from the grunge look of slacker films such as *Reality Bites* and *Dazed and Confused* when plaid was adapted to suit highly fashion-conscious schoolgirls. It helped to set in motion a new fashion for the plaid miniskirt that reflected a playfulness and innocence, but could also be business-like. When the film's costume designer Mona May visited high schools as research, she noticed that baggy plaid shirts were all the rage, so she chose to dress characters in grungy plaid shirts or, for the most fashionable girls, little plaid skirts and jackets. 'We thought of Catholic school, the pleated skirt. But we needed to take it to a higher level and make it high fashion,' she said.

clockwise from top left Burberry scarf at Paris Fashion Week in 2016; Tokyo teenager wearing Burberry check in 2000; style reporter Erica Pelosini outside Burberry during London Fashion Week in 2016.

'We tried red on Alicia and it was really pretty but it wasn't right. We tried blue and it was good, but when we put on the yellow it was like BAM . . . we kept it chic with the little jacket, and went a little Scottish with the big safety pin, but we also have a little midriff showing, to make it a little sexier. And then the stockings. We finished it not with a stiletto but a sensible and girly Mary Jane. It was important to us to keep it real, age appropriate, but still have the characters pop.'[30]

Britney Spears in *Hit Me Baby One More Time*, while not wearing a tartan skirt, helped establish the sexual objectification of the schoolgirl uniform. By the time Britney had become a pop sensation, *Rolling Stone* magazine had announced a new 'Teen Age', with teen spending power reshaping music, films and TV. Britney told the publication that it was she who came up with the idea of school uniforms after vetoing an 'animated Power Ranger-y thing . . . I had this idea where we're in school and bored out of our minds, and we have Catholic uniforms on. And I said, "Why don't we have knee-highs and tie the shirts up to give it a little attitude?"'[31]

It was the influence of Britney Spears, and Russian pop stars t.A.T.u. in 2003, that sparked a trend in Britain for 'naughty schoolgirl' parties, with adults dressed in their plaid skirts and shirts tied around the waist, and which created an uneasy dichotomy between adult erotica and childhood.

BURBERRY CHECK

At the beginning of the millennium, the beige, red and black Burberry check became one of the most recognizable of tartan brands, appearing on bikinis, baseball caps and headscarves, representing 'chav' fashion and shifting it from its original place as an upmarket brand.

Burberry had been founded in 1856 by Thomas Burberry as an outdoor clothing supplier, and during the First World War the company was commissioned to design officers' coats. These trench coats used the signature plaid Burberry lining, and after the war, when the trench coat became popular among middle and upper classes and had two royal warrants assigned to it, a glimpse of this lining was a sign of style and good taste.[32] In the 1990s, a new chief executive, Rose Marie Bravo, shook up the brand by expanding the product line to make it more democratic. Stars such as Victoria Beckham were pictured in the check, which encouraged knock-off imitations on baseball caps and visors. Football casuals were huge fans of European sportswear and British sports brands, and so the Burberry design became linked with this casual style as caps were worn at football matches. Burberry mania reached its peak when British soap star Danniella Westbrook was photographed with her child decked out in Burberry. With the ridicule of this image, Burberry switched its marketing to move back to a more exclusive brand (see page 97).

AL FIT

THING

TARTAN IN STREET STYLE

A guest wears a luxurious tartan coat during New York Fashion Week in 2015.

clockwise from top Teenage fans hold tartan scarves to support Scottish pop group the Bay City Rollers, around 1975; digital editor Miroslava Duma wears a tartan skirt at London Fashion Week spring/summer 2014; fashion buyer and blogger Hilary Tsui wears Toga tartan kilt and Yasbukey handbag at Paris Fashion Week in 2015.

Style in its very meaning refers to the way that we personally choose and combine clothing. It is not aligned to any one design school, particular trend or innovation in fashion. Tartan itself makes an unmistakable statement about individual personal style, evolving throughout history to represent more than geographical and cultural identity. Tartan has also become a subversive fabric, adopted by the punk movement, the Bay City Rollers and pop stars including Madonna who dressed in tartan costumes by Jean Paul Gaultier. Its strong image has been adopted by style tribes who wear its vibrant check to signify allegiance to their peers.

Whilst couture fashion is unattainable for most, everyday street style has become a relevant real-world source of inspiration. The style we see on the street represents an exploration of male and female fashion identities, with tartan used as a rebellious dress code in accordance with particular subcultures. Street style has the power to shape stereotypes and to cause inclusion and exclusion. Its merit is found in its ability to unite people and shape creativity across cultural landscapes.

TARTAN ON THE STREET

The modern wardrobe owes much of its variety to the street-style movements of the past. Male peacocking reached its peak when menswear emerged from relative style obscurity in the mid-twentieth century. Men found their voices among teddy boys, bikers, mods, hippies, skinheads, glam rockers, punks, new romantics, goths and b-boys. Thus when we consider 'modern' fashion it's difficult to find a silhouette or fabric that hasn't been seen before. We might not fully consider the cultural nuances of our clothing but it is likely that every trend we adopt has a history of its own and by wearing a particular garment we are nodding to the heritage of its past.

In the late 1950s and early 1960s, there was a marked cultural shift especially among young men who formed new style communities based on their values and beliefs. This change reflected a slow movement from high culture to popular culture, as class systems became less defined and the wider population developed innovative responses to art, music and fashion. Couture fashion was replaced by ready-to-wear collections with demand shifting from formal clothing to relaxed and comfortable everyday wear. Utilitarian working clothes were popular and as fashion writer Daniele Bott said: 'the couture houses catering for the older, wealthier woman seemed *démodé*, and by the 1970s the new designers were influencing style – they were the *créateurs*, whose inventive grasp of street style established the place of ready-to-wear on the world stage'.[1]

Capturing street style on camera has become the norm, particularly over the last ten years, led by *New York Times* photographer Bill Cunningham and his 'On the Street' column. The origins of street-style photography are thought to rest with Cunningham,

below left A teenager with a mohawk hairstyle wears a typical punk uniform of leather studded jacket and tartan trousers.

right A punk Sex Pistols fan wears tartan trousers with chains and Doc Marten boots.

whose photographs included socialites, celebrities and everyday New Yorkers. Yet capturing famous faces 'off-duty' can be traced back to the 1980s when Amy Arbus photographed rising stars such as Madonna and Anna Sui outside of a contrived studio environment. Her famous image of 'Anthony in a tartan suit', published in *L'Uomo Vogue* in 1981, presented the blurring of several trends in one tartan ensemble with its broad shoulders, pegged trousers, patterned shirt, black army boots, bow tie and cummerbund, which mixed elements of the zoot-suit, tuxedo and rebellious punk uniform into one.

The British punk movement of the late 1970s mixed tartan with leather, ripped nylon and vinyl for an anti-Establishment look that sought to evade class systems. Punks favoured the Stewart tartan, with its subversive historical links, worn ripped, in strips mended with safety pins worn in trouser form or as adapted kilts mirroring the Sex Pistols' cover for *God Save the Queen*, which featured a defaced image of Queen Elizabeth II, used on T-shirts by Vivienne Westwood. As the styles of different tribes became intertwined, a time of cultural change began in Britain. The movement was led by pioneers such as Malcolm McLaren and Vivienne Westwood, and encapsulated music, art and politics. Westwood was a trend leader, mixing tartan with spiked dog collars, safety pins and bondage wear, embodying the style revolution taking place around their Kings Road boutique. Experimentation with tartan and clashing patterns was a powerful statement

with 'people wearing fancy dress and old clothes, just like they did in Paris in 1972 . . . with these clothes, you want to look rakish, you want to look like you can walk down the street feeling like you own it and you're Jack-the-Lad'.[2]

Later the age of the supermodel would welcome a sexier silhouette, led by Gianni Versace who put Cindy Crawford and Helena Christensen on his catwalk. These curvaceous models promoted the trend for bare skin, bra-tops and miniskirts. Young customers snapped up the classic Chanel tweed jacket, styling them with ripped jeans or denim shorts. The allure of the supermodel was counteracted by the grunge look that was inspired by the lumberjack in his plaid shirt. The early 1990s saw Winona Ryder, Johnny Depp and Brad Pitt in grunge tartan, leather and denim that reappeared in 2015 on Cara Delevingne and Rita Ora, who wore tartan shirts, skirts and distressed denim.

Arguably 1995 was the most pivotal year for tartan within popular culture. Immortalized in the 1995 cult classic *Clueless*, the provocative yet innocent tartan style of lead character Cher Horowitz pushed tartan into a new realm of mainstream popular culture still referenced today. She wore tartan as a matching uniform and used it as an identifier to indicate her leadership of a teenage social clique. This schoolgirl look was recreated in 2014 for Australian rapper Iggy Azalea's *Clueless*-inspired music video. *Empire Records* followed the *Clueless* hype in 1995 with Liv Tyler's infamous mini-kilt. The same

clockwise from top left Editor of *Garage* magazine, Michelle Elie, wears Comme des Garçons tartan outfit with Christian Louboutin shoes at Paris Fashion Week in 2014; blogger Aimee Song at Paris Fashion Week in 2015; Jose Cordero in a tartan JMR kilt and Aquascutum blazer jacket, New York Fashion Week autumn/winter 2016.

year Alexander McQueen showcased his Highland Rape collection referencing the Clearances in the 1800s with his original MacQueen red, black and yellow tartan, using Lochcarron tartan and lace found in Brick Lane.

TARTAN AND CELEBRITY

Celebrity culture influences every element of popular dress, filtering through into our wardrobes via the high street. Although steps are being taken to educate the public about the values of provenance and heritage fabrics, shopping culture has shifted from treasuring timeless classics to buying patterns that favour fast-fashion. Twenty-first-century dressing is largely dominated by celebrity-endorsed advertising, and although tartan is a perennial fabric we see its cyclical revival every few years as demand is influenced by celebrity culture and promoted by the media.

American designers such as Tommy Hilfiger and Calvin Klein were some of the first to understand the power of celebrity and its ability to make fashion desirable, by clothing celebrities such as Lenny Kravitz, David Bowie, Usher and Britney Spears. A new generation of tartan wearers were inspired by hip-hop artists such as the Fugees, LL Cool J and Sean 'Puffy' Combs when designer labels and sportswear came together. Later, pleated tartan miniskirts would appear alongside tartan combat trousers worn by singers Avril Lavigne, Gwen Stefani and Black Eyed Peas' Fergie, who epitomized skater-girl style.

The assertion that tartan is 'strictly for extroverts, especially attractive to artists and other free-spirited thinkers who enjoy turning themselves into walking works of art'[3] may have been true twenty years ago but is far from what we see now, particularly in men's fashion where tartan is an integral part of the functional everyday wardrobe. Menswear has become the centre of evolving fashion, with traditionally conservative groups experimenting with grooming, clothing and accessories.

The tartan shirt was first made popular by university students in the 1950s, who bought into the affordable, relaxed aesthetic, seeing tartan as the most masculine of fabrics. Later on, in the 1980s, punks would wear tartan shirts tied around their waists with jeans or shorts. Seeking to avoid fashion norms, followers of the grunge movement wore garments with subversive undertones. Later the tartan shirt became an unofficial symbol of the 1990s' music scene fuelled by the rise of bands such as Nirvana and Pearl Jam. Often seen on purveyors of indie music, the tartan shirt has filtered through the contemporary music world too, worn by everyone from Fleet Foxes to Kings of Leon.

Today the modern hipster has inadvertently formed a new style clique that began in Brooklyn and spread to London, where value and authenticity became integral to the way they chose their clothes. The idea of national identity and of 'Britishness' - in its social codes of conduct and the movement of class systems – were integral to the hipster trend. Tommy Hilfiger, a purveyor of plaid, believes

that the flannel shirt is 'always appropriate for being outdoors in the city or the country . . . worn as overshirts over a turtle neck or a Henley but most authentic with corduroys or jeans and boots'.[4]

On the high-street, Topman reported in 2010 that tartan shirt sales had increased by 49 per cent from the previous year, selling an equivalent of four tartan shirts every minute.[5] Certainly this universal appeal meant that the checked shirt evaded class divisions and, with the development of social media and a demand for style documentation, the doors of fashion houses, glossy magazines and private wardrobes have simultaneously opened, allowing transatlantic tartan wearers to find inspiration from other cities and cultures and form style communities based on their similar dress codes. The heritage revival that arrived in 2011 popularized garments associated with the traditional British countryside and was appropriated by celebrities at music festivals. It also marked renewed interest in associated brands such as Barbour and Hunter. Tartan itself has been a consistent festival staple from Gwen Stefani's grunge trousers when No Doubt played Glastonbury in 2002 to footballers' wives who wore their tartan with Hunter wellingtons. Now, looser groups are forming online as a result of the modern street-style movement, as like-minded individuals see similarities within their dress. With the arrival of Instagram in 2013, dressing for the camera was paramount, as people grouped together in style communities and social media became intertwined

left Singer Gwen Stefani wears trademark tartan trousers at Scotland's T in the Park music festival, 2002.

above Casey Wescott, Christian Wargo, Robin Pecknold, Skye Skjelset, J. Tillman of Fleet Foxes in San Francisco, 2008.

with our everyday lives. As part of that consciousness about the reach of photography and the desire for self-expression, communities have appeared that seek to 'reinvigorate perceptions of Scotland', showing that the creation of tartan from sheep to shelf is uniquely Scottish. According to Gordon Millar, the founder of Scot Street Style, an online community that promotes Scottish national identity: 'We are curious by nature and people-watching is a pastime we all participate in. High fashion runway shows exclude most of us, but when someone walks by us on the street we can actively admire their style.'[6]

In that respect street style today is about communicating the general attitude or lifestyle of the wearer rather than necessarily broadcasting a political or philosophical message. Trends are now dictated by social networking and the sharing of fashion-related content has meant that, when the cyclical interest in tartan reappears, it is quickly adopted by people on the street. Street-style photographer James Bent suggests that: 'The latest looks from the runway and street photographs from fashion weeks proves a powerful incentive, inspiring people to express themselves through clothing, reassess their wardrobes and strive to improve their style.'[7]

TARTAN IN CONTEMPORARY FASHION

A model walks the runway at CND for The Blonds spring/summer 2015, New York.

right Supermodel Naomi Campbell in a dramatic Vivienne Westwood tartan dress and mini kilt, 1994.

far right Alice Dellal models at the Vivienne Westwood Red Label show for London Fashion Week spring/summer 2016/2017.

Tartan is a quality, enduring fabric that has experienced longevity in the fashion industry to become a wardrobe staple and a recurring catwalk trend that filters down on to the high street. Leading cultural change for more than three decades, Vivienne Westwood's rebellious use of tartan placed the fabric at the forefront of British consciousness throughout the 1970s and beyond. Later, fellow tartan visionary Alexander McQueen became known for his exquisite tailoring of the MacQueen tartan, which he created to honour his ancestors.

TARTAN VISIONARIES

Vivienne Westwood

Known for her parodies of the British aristocracy, skilful revisions of historical dress and her eccentric approach to fashion, Vivienne Westwood has used tartan to create beautifully tailored womenswear collections that have allowed her to transition from figurehead of the punk movement to darling of the Establishment. During this process she has transformed tartan in fashion from something conservative into cutting-edge design.

Westwood's most notable tartan collection – Anglomania autumn/winter 1993/1994 – merged her fascination with both English and Scottish tradition. It marked the debut of the MacAndreas tartan named after Westwood's husband Andreas Kronthaler, which was produced by Lochcarron of Scotland. Supermodels Linda Evangelista, Christy Turlington, Naomi Campbell and Kate Moss wore a full collection of cropped tartan mohair jackets, mini-kilts and belted plaids with jaunty, pheasant-feather tam o' shanters. Moss was powerful in a silk taffeta MacAndreas tartan ballgown, but it was fellow supermodel Naomi Campbell who stole the show when she fell off her 25cm/10in, blue mock-croc platforms on to the catwalk beneath her.

Westwood's body-shaping aesthetic was developed in the mid-1980s with the 'mini-crini', a reworking of the nineteenth-century crinoline often worn with a tailored jacket, bustle and platform shoes. This highly tailored signature was prominent in her Harris Tweed 1987/1988 show (see page 138), which embraced the curvaceous female form, exaggerating the bust and moving away from the padded masculine shoulders of the time. The Statue of Liberty corset became one of Westwood's most iconic designs, pushing the chest upwards and cinching the waist. It was worn with the mini-crini sculptural crinoline skirt, which widened the hips, creating the perfect hourglass shape. In November 1989 Westwood's first British *Vogue* cover showed model Tatjana Patitz in an Ancient Bruce of Kinnaird tartan jacket, which was 'deemed the star of the season's winter dressing . . . It combined bias cutting, curved seamlines, signature gilt buttons, velvet collar and cuffs.'[1]

Westwood's tartan designs have often referenced urban environments such as London-inspired 'McBrick' and 'McStone' as well as traditional elements of Scottish dress. In Dressing Up 1991/1992, which Westwood presented in Azzedine Alaïa's Parisian atelier, there were 'tartans, sporrans and lace jabots – alongside fake-fur leopard skin coats, elongated scarlet-toned beefeater hats and mackintoshes embellished with old master prints'.[2]

One of Westwood's most prolific patrons, Romilly McAlpine, showcased a collection of her garments at a Museum of London exhibition in 2000, which celebrated Westwood's ability to manipulate tweeds and 'draw up wildly different patterns'.[3] Following suit, the Victoria & Albert Museum held a much wider Westwood retrospective in 2004, while in 2006 *Anglomania: Tradition and Transgression in British Fashion* opened at the Metropolitan Museum of Art in New York.

Alexander McQueen

Despite his untimely death aged just forty, Alexander McQueen was one of Britain's most celebrated designers, known for the extraordinary depth of his research and an ability to make historical themes relevant for a contemporary audience. His lifelong muse – Isabella Blow – described McQueen's work as 'sabotage and tradition – all the things that the 1990s represented'.[4] These contradicting themes were

The Vivienne Westwood Red Label show at London Fashion Week autumn/winter 2014/2015.

pivotal in McQueen's designs and were married with clanship and ancestry for Highland Rape (1995/1996) and The Widows of Culloden (2006/2007), in which McQueen used the powerful black, red and yellow MacQueen tartan to communicate his reaction to Scotland's turbulent history. His exclusive use of the family sett (produced by Lochcarron of Scotland) represented the personal resonance of this collection for McQueen and his deep connection with Scottish costume.

Although controversial in its title (which critics thought advocated violence against women), the Highland Rape collection was a result of McQueen's research into the cruelty that eighteenth-century Highlanders suffered at the hands of British government forces following the Jacobite rebellions and their subsequent migrations. Presented in collaboration with the British Fashion Council at London's Natural History Museum in 1995, the show's grisly title was echoed in the slashed garments and dazed models who staggered down a runway scattered with heather and bracken, appearing to have experienced extreme trauma. Some attendees identified strains of misogyny in McQueen's designs and were disturbed by the forcefully exposed skin beneath the slashed clothing. For McQueen the collection acted as a relevant protest against the treatment of his ancestors during the Highland Clearances. 'Scotland for me is a harsh, cold and bitter place,' said McQueen. 'It was even worse when my great, great grandfather used to live there . . . I hate it when people romanticize Scotland. There's nothing romantic about its history.'[5] Victoria and Albert Museum curator Kate Bethune accepted the designer's intention to rebel against the romanticized notion of Scottish history: 'McQueen's models were not victims but powerful women who, in their ripped and torn clothes, represented the survival of Highland women during the "rape" of their communities by the English.'[6] In McQueen's words the collection: 'was a shout against English designers doing flamboyant Scottish clothes. My father's family originates from the Isle of Skye and I'd studied the history of the Scottish upheavals and the Clearances. People were so unintelligent they thought this was about women being raped – yet Highland Rape was about England's rape of Scotland.'[7]

With its bold sett of rich red and black check with fine yellow stripes, McQueen used his tartan to trim jackets and figure-fitting bodices covered with slashed lace. The fabric was initially bought by Detmar Blow, the husband of McQueen's muse Isabella Blow, to help the cash-poor designer realize his vision. McQueen used it to make dresses, bustles, suits, skirts and the infamous 'bumster' trousers. According to McQueen the base of the spine was an erotic part of the body and his fascination with lengthening the female torso was the inspiration behind these risqué trousers that

far left Alexander McQueen catwalk, the London Collections: Men autumn/winter 2014.

left Alexander McQueen tartan dress at Paris Fashion Week autumn/winter 2006/2007.

were cut seductively low on the hip to expose the length of the body from the neck to lower spine. A key talking point of the Highland Rape collection, the 'bumster' became one of McQueen's signatures and sparked the low-rise jeans trend that was popular throughout the 1990s.

McQueen's attachment to his Scottish heritage was evident throughout his work. The very obvious occupation with Scots history seen in Highland Rape and The Widows of Culloden was referenced more subtly in his Joan of Arc (1998/1999) and The Girl Who Lived in a Tree (2008/2009) collections. In The Widows of Culloden, which came ten years after his controversial Highland Rape, McQueen's revised tartan garments now portrayed nobility and refinement and were paired with regal pheasant feather headpieces. It was a softer representation of McQueen's national pride, with models appearing in interpretations of the early *fèileadh-mòr* and more recognizably modern versions of the contemporary kilt, with tartan draped around embroidered nude linings. Exploring both peasant and upper-class dress, McQueen followed a well-explored narrative of neutral tweeds and feathers and later a beautifully draped, one-shoulder MacQueen tartan dress was softened with a tulle underskirt and structured with a thick black belt to cinch the waist. The MacQueen tartan was equally enticing in skinny trouser suits with nods to traditional Highland dress, which presented the designer's refined craftsmanship at its very best. It was a collection full of grandeur yet an obvious reaction against the romanticized view of Scotland portrayed by fellow designers. Criticizing Vivienne Westwood, who McQueen said 'makes tartan lovely and romantic and tries to pretend that's how it was', the designer was adamant that a realistic portrayal of eighteenth-century Scotland did not involve 'beautiful women drifting across the moors in swathes of unmanageable chiffon.'[8]

McQueen's showpiece tartan, tulle and lace one-shoulder dress made a red-carpet appearance later that year worn by actress Sarah Jessica Parker when she accompanied McQueen to the Metropolitan Museum of Art gala dinner to celebrate the launch of *Anglomania: Tradition and Transgression in British Fashion*. McQueen wore a *fèileadh-mòr* and tailcoat in his own tartan with an oversized sporran.

TRANSATLANTIC TARTAN

Burberry

Synonymous with British culture, it's no surprise that Burberry epitomizes heritage fashion. At the very core of the brand we find the rich narrative of the signature trench coat, worn by British soldiers during the First World War and earlier by Sir Ernest Shackleton during his Antarctic expeditions. Famed for its distinctive check, Burberry has used tartan in varying degrees throughout its 160-year history, experiencing both fortune and farce depending on its potency.

'Tartan has a purpose in every walk of life.' Tommy Hilfiger

According to the official Scottish Register of Tartans, Burberry's distinctive check, called Haymarket Check after the company's flagship store in London, was originally created by an Italian luggage company. Reportedly, the tartan became so intertwined with the Burberry brand that the retailer trademarked it in 1924 as a corporate tartan, titled Burberry (Genuine).

Used in the lining of Burberry's iconic trench coat, this subtle design detail remained hidden for almost fifty years until, in 1967, the company expanded its accessories and featured the check itself on umbrellas, luggage and scarves. Apparently, the Burberry tartan scarf came about because of a window-dressing mishap, when a signature Burberry trench coat was turned inside out on a mannequin revealing the tartan check print. Customers then began to request the tartan version so Burberry started making products that featured the check more prominently.

Armed with a royal warrant from Queen Elizabeth II and capitalizing on its British image, the company expanded into Asian and American markets. However, Burberry's traditional image was seen as passé, so a subsequent rebranding exercise was set in motion in the 1990s, which focused heavily on lower-priced merchandise featuring bold Burberry check.

Tartan can, however, become over-exposed, and Burberry became associated with anti-fashion when the check was adopted by football 'casuals' and 'chavs' as a badge of honour. Tarnished by its link to these social groups, the Burberry tartan was further damaged by the mass of counterfeit goods flooding the marketplace as 'chav' culture flourished. Blighted by its own success and at the height of these image problems, rap group Goldie Lookin Chain were presented with a Vauxhall Cavalier covered in Burberry check, dubbed the 'Chavalier'. Burberry ordered that the car was destroyed, citing copyright infringement. At a time when the brand was accessible and affordable to all it became associated with anti-social behaviour, a far cry from founder Thomas Burberry's respectable beginnings in 1856. Ironically, the company's newest image was hugely bolstered by a series of high-profile advertising campaigns featuring Romeo Beckham, son of David and Victoria, who had once been branded the poster couple of celebrity 'chavdom' by the British media.

The twenty-first century saw the rebirth of brand Burberry, shedding elements of its conservative style and courting a free-spirited, youthful market with a contemporary brand overhaul. The year 2006 marked a turning point for Burberry when CEO Angela Ahrendts and creative director Christopher Bailey joined forces to turn the company's fortunes around. Bailey is credited with reinventing the company's infamous check, completely deconstructing and recreating the pattern to attract the brand's privileged target customer and push Burberry's digital offering.

After taking the helm in 2014 as both CEO and chief creative officer, Bailey confidently led

Laura Bailey arrives at Burberry Prorsum spring/summer show at London Fashion Week in 2011.

Britain's leading luxury label back to its prestigious roots. Despite being accepted by the brand's desired aristocratic and celebrity customer base – Kate Middleton, Gwyneth Paltrow and Keira Knightley – its most consistent consumer on home turf is the foreign tourist. The burgeoning Chinese middle class and a steady stream of Japanese and American customers desire British-made goods and are unfazed or unaware of the 'chav-check' furore of years past. The Japanese in particular are talented at restyling a traditional fabric in contemporary ways 'channelling an energy and drive for creative freedom, making distinct fashion and style statements that scream innovation and individuality'.[9]

Tartan has reappeared at the forefront of Burberry's contemporary repertoire once again: for example in February 2016 in a striking women's checked coat made from brushed tartan wool mohair offset with thick black seams. Continuing with its ambitions to capture a millennial market, Burberry announced that from September 2016 it will follow a direct-to-consumer model, with collections shown at London Fashion Week available to buy immediately following the show.

Ralph Lauren

Like the Ralph Lauren brand itself, the high-quality American 'preppy' look has mass appeal. Made popular in the 1960s, this distinguished style has become symbolic of a nation that evaded changing fashion trends in favour of a smart, educated look,

Cotton chambray trousers, jacket and cotton shirt all by Ralph Lauren, *Glamour* magazine, 1973.

later to become a menswear classic. Inspired by the quintessential British country weekend with references to American cowboys and sporting activities, Lauren has endured ever-changing fashion whims by cleverly staying true to the all-American, ready-to-wear aesthetic of plaid shirts and denim.

This dominant American fashion house is known for reinventing a period in history for a contemporary audience and has taken much inspiration from across the Atlantic over the years – often quipped as 'doing the British look better than the British do'. Inspired by royalty and the British upper classes, Lauren was intrigued by the Duke and Duchess of Windsor: 'not just the perfection of cut that characterized all the duke's clothes, even at their most casual; it was the extremely relaxed way in which he wore them. No matter what the occasion, he never looked like a tailor's dummy. The clothes never dominated the man.'[10]

Majoring in classic nostalgia, some say Lauren's greatest achievement was 'selling Englishness to the British'.[11] His beginnings on the shop floor selling ties gave Lauren a unique perspective of his whole business, allowing him to consider his full commercial offering in addition to specific design details. Despite critics attributing his achievements to clever marketing rather than design acumen, 'it took an American Jew of Russian descent – Ralph Lauren – to commodify that look into something that could be worn by men, women, Brits, Yanks, and every other variation on gender, nationality and persuasion.'[12]

The country endeavours of the English gent were emulated in the hunting jacket, the sports jersey and the checked shirt – favourites that gave Lauren long-term success by understanding the customers' appetite for relaxed, comfortable sportswear. He told fashion historian Colin McDowell: 'When I look at tartan for a new season, I always feel that I'm rediscovering it. Of course, it doesn't change. What changes are the different ways we can look at it. Its appeal is almost endless. That, to me, is why people connect so well with tartan, why it's recognizable to everybody.'[13]

THE KILT

Whether teamed with a T-shirt or leather jacket, kilts are as acceptable worn casually as they are for formal occasions. The new generation of kilt wearers includes actors Ewan McGregor and Samuel L. Jackson, whose respective adoption of the kilt reflects the widespread acceptance of this national dress among locals and non-Scots. The contemporary reimagining of the kilt has kept the design relevant in the ever-changing world of fashion with innovative kilt-makers creating exciting new versions of this iconic national dress.

French designer Jean Paul Gaultier's signature style of Breton striped top, tartan kilt and biker boots marks his desire to push the powerful visual appeal of the kilt to its limits. When photographed for French

below left Jean Paul Gaultier show at the Fashion Forward event in New York, 2011.

right A sketch and fabric swatches by Isaac Mizrahi for the Extreme Kilt strapless cashmere dress, autumn 1989.

Elle in 1994 we saw Gaultier in this uniform, blurring national identities between the tartan kilt and the striped shirt worn by sailors in the French navy, as powerful to the French as the kilt is to Scots. On his fascination with skirts for men Gaultier commented: 'Throughout history many virile men have worn skirts, from samurais to Scots, who have always worn kilts. I don't believe that fabrics have a gender any more than certain garments do. I've always presented the skirt in a very masculine way, on very "manly" models wearing thick black socks and heavy boots.'[14] Gaultier himself has worn daring micro-kilts that fall much higher than the traditional knee-grazing version. Experimenting with the idea of men in skirts throughout the 1980s and 1990s, Gaultier moved from kilts to sarongs and maxi-skirts. At his Paris Fashion Week show in 2014, he sent older models down the runway in punk outfits made of leather and tartan, accessorized with mohawks.

American designer Tommy Hilfiger is also known for showing tartan or 'plaid' kilts with sports socks and tough boots, although his highly commercial aesthetic is the complete opposite of Gaultier's flesh-flashing skirts. A leader of casual dressing, Hilfiger has featured kilts in both his men's and women's collections for several years, thereby toughening the all-American fraternity look with some essential British edge. A Hilfiger advertising campaign for autumn/winter 1997/1998 showed 'a group of multi-ethnic men existing in a kind of edenic space of homo-camaraderie. The models were depicted

STRAPLESS
CASHMERE
KILT
LINDA
62

Contemporary kilts by Samantha McCoach of Le Kilt, inspired by her grandmother who was a traditional kilt maker.

wearing their kilts with plaid shirts and workboots, thus combining two stereotypes of masculinity, the Highlander and the Lumberjack.'[15] According to Hilfiger: 'Tartan has a purpose in every walk of life. It really rocks on stage from Bill Haley and His Comets to the Bay City Rollers and Rod Stewart all the way to the Sex Pistols.'[16]

When tartan is represented in chiffon, fine cashmere or silk it becomes an entirely new entity. Isaac Mizrahi's 'extreme kilt' for autumn/winter 1989/1990 converted the traditional kilt shape into a long Stewart tartan cashmere flannel gown complete with bodice buckles. Inspired by the pleats of a traditional kilt, Mizrahi described this work with tartan as 'the best collection of my life. It was my hilarious American take on England and Scotland.' On a visit to Scotland Mizrahi had a kilt made and 'liked knowing everything about it then being able to absolutely destroy this knowledge.'[17] Similarly the leather panels of Azzedine Alaïa's women's kilts for autumn/winter 2000/2001 also subverted the traditional view of the kilt, and even Japanese label Comme des Garçons featured the kilt in their autumn/winter 2012/2013 show alongside a red checked suit. From Japanese designer Jun Takahashi in 2000 covering models from head to toe in tartan to Marc Jacobs's show for Louis Vuitton in autumn/winter 2004/2005 which was described as 'Tim Burton's view of the Highlands', kilts have been realized in different textiles by international designers and altered throughout the twenty-first century but never beyond recognition.

With a strong interest in their native tartan, young Scottish designers have put their twist on traditional Highland dress. Edinburgh-based Howie Nicholsby of 21st Century Kilts leads the charge for contemporary kilt design. Founded in 1996, Nicholsby's kilts are made in alternative fabrics including tweed, denim and leather, and they feature detachable pockets for cash, cards and mobile phones, thereby presenting the kilt as a practical garment for everyday wear.

While some kilt designers have distanced themselves from clan tartans, newcomers such as Samantha McCoach of Le Kilt are drawing on traditional kilt-making heritage to create something contemporary. Women's kilts have been modernized by McCoach, who founded Le Kilt in 2014 and has capitalized on family tradition by bringing her designs to life at the Lochcarron and Hainsworth mills. Traditionalists often advise against mixing tartans, yet McCoach's blend of Black Watch, Wallace Red and Morgan tartans is a refreshing alternative to standard kilt designs. Her original collection of twelve kilts in different colours of tartan used the classic colours of the Black Watch – solid black, green and navy, which she identifies with classic style. Citing tartan's 'subcultural power' as a key selling point for 'reinventing part of the national identity'[18] McCoach styles the kilt in a contemporary way, thereby creating a product that generations of women want to wear.

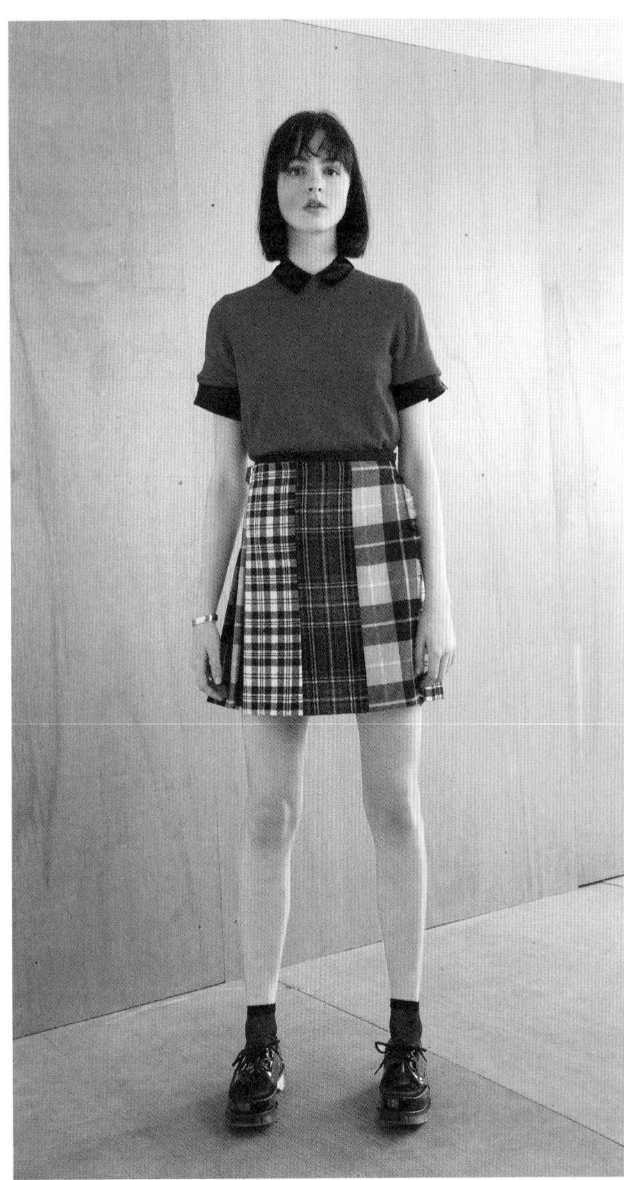

K. M. K. Ltd.
INACLETE MILL
Mix No. 5015
Batch No. 782
Grist 15c
Colour

THE ORIGINS OF TWEED

A bale of blended wool tagged with mix and batch numbers at Kenneth Mackenzie Mill in Stornoway, Isle of Lewis.

Enriched by the history and traditions that define its processes, tweed is a physical embodiment of the landscape where it is woven. Typically seen with a multicoloured herringbone design, tweed patterns have traditionally taken inspiration from the wild, barren landscape and scenery of Scotland and the earthy colours of the heather and gorse. With its own legislation and definitive stamp, Harris Tweed is a fabric like no other, known for its durability against both the heat and the cold simultaneously – a vital characteristic for life on the isolated, windswept Scottish isles. Meanwhile Borders tweed has a rich local history, emerging in the eighteenth century fuelled by industrial revolution, and is often connected with the aristocracy and wealthy sporting estates.

EARLY HARRIS TWEED

For hundreds of years the people of the Outer Hebrides survived solely on the land they called home, taking wool from their sheep to make tweed that was hardy enough to withstand the everyday rigours of island life. Early seventeenth-century tweed production is firmly rooted at the door of the independent weavers who made the fabric to clothe and protect themselves and their families from extreme weather conditions. Found only in the Outer Hebridean Isles of Lewis, Harris, Uist and Barra, the original tweed was domestically produced, and any surplus cloth was traded among the islanders like a form of currency.

Harris Tweed was originally known as *clo-mòr* (big cloth) and was a combination of spun wool died with heather, dandelion and other native plants. At the beginning of the summer (normally June) sheep would be sheared. To give the cloth its rough texture the wool came from different breeds - Scottish cross-breeds and Cheviot sheep being the most common. The wool was washed in water and dipped in soap solution, then left to dry outside.

In the days before machinery could ease the process, Harris Tweed was produced by crofters using laborious and physically demanding methods. Traditionally the

left A remote cottage with a red roof on the Isle of Harris, photographed in the spring.

above left and right The textures and colours of the rugged island landscape have shaped the composition of Harris Tweed.

wool was hand-dipped in urine to fix the dye and carded between flat boards with wire teeth, which groups of women would scrape together to separate any knots. The wool had a tough consistency after spinning so it was manipulated over a trestle framework and soaked in a urine solution again. Life became much less arduous for the women of Harris when the spinning wheel appeared in the early eighteenth century, allowing yarn to be wound on to bobbins and set up on a loom.

EARLY BORDERS TWEED

Developed in the eighteenth century, the Borders tweed industry was largely focused around the towns of Hawick and Selkirk where the mills appeared during the Industrial Revolution. Mill workers typically worked six days a week beginning at 6 a.m. Dirty fleeces came into the mill and had to be cleaned to remove any contamination. The wool was sorted before being teased and carded, converting the fibres into usable lengths of wool to be sent out of the mill to the spinners and later to the weavers. Once the cloth had been woven it was sent back to the mill to be finished.

In addition to the favourable geographic landmarks of the Borders, such as the River Tweed, which facilitated mill manufacturing, the native Borders' Cheviot sheep provided the raw wool required to supply the surrounding mills. The close proximity of the mills to the River Tweed is often connected to the fabric's name 'tweed' and incorrectly attributed to the cloth's origin.

During the 1840s Borders tweed entered a new phase of growth, when it was discovered by the aristocracy on hunting trips to Scotland. The upper classes wanted to emulate Queen Victoria and Prince Albert so English noblemen began to buy Scottish estates and in turn brought tweed back to their London tailors to make suits. After Prince Albert first leased Balmoral in 1848, he designed the Balmoral tweed exclusively for the estate. Wealthy Victorians wanted to follow Highland traditions and provide clothing for their staff so 'estate tweeds' were used to identify people who lived and worked in the same area. Blended colours were introduced to camouflage clothes used in hunting, fishing and shooting, allowing for greater variety in patterns. Lady Dunmore's influence in the

left, above and below A worker operating a modern high speed machine in the warping department at the Wilson and Glenny Mill at Hawick in the Scottish Borders, 1949; Workers outside the Wilson and Glenny Mill, 1950.

1840s introduced Harris Tweed to the British aristocracy and before long every sporting estate had its own tweed. Rich estate owners requested distinctive patterns and took inspiration from the land with even the brightest patterns designed to blend in with the heather, timber and rocky terrain. The Border's rich and diverse textile heritage flourished and by a century later nearly one-third of the Borders' labour force was employed in the industry.[1] The American market also fuelled this period of commercial boom, importing large amounts of Scottish tweed throughout the nineteenth century. However, a new tax on woollen imports brought into America made these shipments less cost-effective, and Borders tweed fell out of fashion until Serbian textile designer and painter Bernat Klein fuelled its revival in the 1960s and 1970s.

Klein revived Borders tweed by supplying fabric from Scotland to haute couture designers around the world. His weaving factory was based in Galashiels, from where he created innovative textiles including vibrant mohair and tweed. He built up a steady commercial trade and enticed European designers such as Coco Chanel in 1962 to chose Klein's fabrics for her spring collection. This led to subsequent orders from Dior, Balenciaga, Pierre Cardin and Saint Laurent. Contemporary fashion houses continue to use tweed from the Borders and Outer Hebrides and, while they manipulate the fabric to suit modern trends, the cloth retains its heritage.

THE DUNMORE FAMILY AND NINETEENTH-CENTURY HARRIS TWEED

Often positioned as father of the Harris Tweed industry, Alexander Murray succeeded his late father in 1836 to become the sixth Earl of Dunmore. Before the earl's unexpected death in 1845 (in a horse-riding accident), it is thought that he had the foresight to order lengths of tweed to be woven in the Murray tartan to create uniforms for his tenants on the Harris estate. This began an onslaught of business that marked the beginning of the Harris Tweed industry. With the onset of the industrial age came cultural change, and Harris Tweed proved pivotal to the Hebrides' economic survival. Earlier, in the mid-eighteenth century, there had been an increase in rent and rates across Harris, with landowners demanding cash settlements rather than accepting payment in produce from the tenant's land. Unable to meet rising rates, many crofters had been forced to leave their homes.

Local history suggests that after his death Alexander's wife, Catherine Murray, Lady Dunmore, took over responsibility for the estate, saw an opportunity to sell Harris Tweed and first brought it to the attention of commercial markets. Although it is difficult to pinpoint whether Alexander had begun to promote Harris Tweed significantly before his death or whether Lady Dunmore masterminded the enterprise on her own, it's clear that she was instrumental in developing the fabric and reinvigorating a sustainable local industry.

clockwise from top left Yarn is wound on to bobbins and will form the basis of the warp (vertical threads) and weft (horizontal threads); wool is dyed in stainless steel drums that mix an exact recipe of natural dyes and fixing chemicals; an infinite number of colours can be achieved with wool that is dyed before being spun.

During the economic difficulties of the Highland potato famine of 1846–7, when the islanders were struggling to maintain a fragile economy, Lady Dunmore established that selling Harris Tweed was a viable commercial business. Recognizing its sales potential, she set up an embroidery school in 1849 and saw an opportunity to market tweed to the gentry in London, after having Harris Tweed jackets made for her own staff. Two local sisters were sent to Alloa to learn advanced weaving techniques, and they introduced their skills to the island on their return. A group of Lady Dunmore's staff began to produce garments for the aristocracy, who wore the tweed while playing sports.

The word 'tweed' itself is said to be the result of a misunderstanding between a Hawick factory and a London merchant in the nineteenth century. When 'Messrs William Watson and Son' sent a selection of 'tweels' to Mr James Locke, the latter misread the factory invoice, reading the word 'tweel' as 'tweed'. It is unclear whether this account is accurate but there is no doubt that the newly branded fabric could also benefit from an association with the River Tweed and the Scottish Borders. It soon became a fashionable, quality fabric among the Victorian upper classes, and Lady Dunmore secured the royal seal of approval, which substantially boosted tweed sales.

During the last years of the nineteenth century the Harris Tweed industry greatly benefited from the support of the Duchess of Sutherland and Lady Seaforth Mackenzie, who promoted the Highland home industries within affluent social circles. However, Harris Tweed's popularity encouraged copycats and, by then, cheaper versions of the fabric were being manufactured, which made the long-term survival of the tweed industry in the Outer Hebrides uncertain.

THE HARRIS TWEED ASSOCIATION AND TRADEMARK

Keen to protect local industry merchants, it was decided that a certification stamp was needed to differentiate Harris Tweed from other woven fabrics. The 1905 Trademarks Act made it possible for 'standardization' marks to be registered. In a bid to protect Harris Tweed from imitations, the fabric was given protection status in 1909, when a law was passed signifying that the Harris Tweed orb mark could represent fabric only authentically spun, dyed and handwoven on the islands of the Outer Hebrides. The Harris Tweed Association was also founded that year, to bring greater regulation to the industry. It was reported that the orb was inspired by the Dunmore family crest of an orb and a Maltese cross, but Lady Anne Dunmore has since confirmed that these reports were inaccurate.

Subsequently, the newly formed Harris Tweed Association Ltd made an application for registration of the orb as a trademark in 1910. The design featured a globe surrounded by a cross with the words 'Harris Tweed' followed by 'Made in Harris', 'Made in Lewis' or 'Made in Uist', depending on the origins of the cloth. This was done despite a dispute from some Harris traders who opposed

above left Harris Tweed was once solely produced from the wool of Hebridean Blackface sheep on the Isles of Lewis and Harris.

left Yarns for the warp and weft arrive from the mill to the weaver's home and are threaded on to the loom by hand.

The word 'tweed' is said to be the result of a misunderstanding between a Hawick factory and a London merchant in the nineteenth century, when the latter misread the word 'tweel' as 'tweed'.

tweed production in their neighbouring islands. Official stamping of the cloth with the trademark began in 1911. The accompanying definition of the fabric stated: 'Harris Tweed means a tweed hand-spun and handwoven and dyed by the crofter and cottars in the Outer Hebrides.'

The foresight to protect the fabric with a trademark certainly paved the way for the Harris Tweed industry's modern success story. Chief Executive of the Harris Tweed Authority Lorna Macaulay credits these 'early pioneers who set up the Harris Tweed Association during a very difficult socio-economic climate, who had the vision to register a trademark for a fledgling industry.'[2]

PRE-WAR TWEED

With the trademark in place across the Outer Hebrides, production of Harris Tweed soared. Yet despite the demand, the quality of the fabric was ambiguous and the Harris Tweed Association found it difficult to monitor the mark and attribute the term 'Harris Tweed' to fabrics that did not meet the necessary requirements.

While the demand for tweed was reaching a crescendo, the island of Lewis experienced a brief slump from 1911 to 1912, largely because of overproduction. The tweed industry provided a livelihood for much of its population, with the irregularity of the fishing industry forcing local men into weaving. The introduction of a tweed inspector to Lewis greatly increased its fortunes, with an inspector present to verify the quality and credibility of the fabric. A debate on the merits of hand-spun versus mill-spun cloth reached its height in 1912-1913, with a report into the topic stating: 'The durability of a cloth made of pure wool lies in the amount of twist given to the yarn in spinning. A machine can impart any amount of twist to yarn, but, in practice, each additional turn of the machine increases the costs of production, and therefore the tendency is for the manufacturer to diminish the quantity of twist.'[3]

Standards slipped in a bid to meet demand, and the combination of poor fibre quality and careless weaving resulted in poorly produced tweed that damaged the reputation of the Harris Tweed brand. With the outbreak of the First World War in 1914 came the loss of a large proportion of the male workforce, so attempts to streamline processes within the Harris Tweed industry were understandably static until after the war.

By the 1920s conflict between hand-spun and mill-spun yarn had died down, with much of the yarn being imported from the mainland. Large parts of Harris Tweed production were becoming mainland based, with the mills taking over all processes apart from the traditional handweaving done in the islander's homes to meet the minimum requirements necessary to obtain the Harris Tweed stamp. By that time the Scottish Borders textile industry was in decline. The town of Galashiels had lost 635 men during the First World War, many in a single attack in Gallipoli. Several of the mill-owners' sons were among the casualties, and as a result many of the mills had no natural successors, and companies were taken over by outsiders.

HARRIS TWEED
HAND WOVEN IN THE OUTER HEBRIDES
CERTIFICATION TRADE MARK

THE FALL + RISE OF HARRIS TWEED

The finished tweed is examined by the Harris Tweed Authority, then an orb mark is ironed on to the reverse of the fabric.

right above Every Harris Tweed pattern has its own characteristics and on closer inspection the depth of colour within each thread is revealed.

right below Before mechanical rollers teased and mixed the wool, it was carded by hand using flat backed wooden paddles.

Harris Tweed is one of few traditional textiles to achieve cult status. Still woven by hand in the Outer Hebrides, the fabric has real value in a world of mass production. Over the course of its history the Harris Tweed industry has experienced several sustained periods of boom and bust. Despite facing near extinction, the fabric survived its lean years and has benefited from a fashionable revival, in the process helping to boost the flagging economy of the Western Isles.

REPOSITIONING TWEED

The Harris Tweed industry experienced substantial upheaval over the years from its peak in 1960, when more than 900 weavers were employed in the industry, to 2009 when production reached a low of 0.5 million metres/0.55 million yards. When comparing this figure to a recorded peak production of 6.4 million metres/7.6 million yards in 1966, a picture is painted of industrial instability.

Throughout the 1980s and 1990s the industry was damaged by mass production of tweed internationally that capitalized on the Harris Tweed name but had no alliance to the islands of its origin. The reworked Board of Trade definition that Harris Tweed was 'a tweed made from pure virgin wool produced in Scotland, spun, dyed and finished in the Outer Hebrides and handwoven by the islanders at their own homes'[1] placed greater restrictions on the use of the Harris Tweed name and the processes involved in making it, yet the brand itself was still being exploited. Imports from the Far East and low labour rates meant that genuine Harris Tweed was an expensive commodity at the top end of the market while cheap imports threatened to overthrow the industry, even though these imports couldn't legally carry the Harris Tweed brand name.

While attempting to police the use of the Harris Tweed name, the industry was also suffering from a decline in demand that escalated in the mid-1980s with the collapse of the North American market. Price wars between the mills led to a fall in sales, with some businesses favouring short-term profit over long-term gain. For more than fifty years North America had been the biggest export market for the cloth and, with the fabric's most loyal customer gone, the tweed industry fell into disarray. From employing half the island's population to barely keeping a handful in work, the mills struggled to survive, weavers were living on the breadline and many were forced to leave the islands to find alternative employment.

As production became more volatile and exhibited a serious downward trajectory, drastic action was required to restructure and modernize the industry. Repositioning Harris Tweed as a desirable product with help from national and EU funding allowed the industry to remain afloat, but economic pressure throughout the mid and late 1980s 'underlined the fragility of the island's economy and its dependence on the declining fortunes of Harris Tweed'.[2] The industry's outlook was

summarized well in 1990 by Duncan Martin, chairman of the Development Working Party that was created by the Harris Tweed Association to promote a five-year industry regeneration strategy: 'The world is no longer beating a path to our door to buy Harris Tweed. We have to change, adapt, evolve to satisfy the present-day marketplace or pay the price.'[3] The report cited a declining market, the loss of American custom, old-fashioned weaving equipment, which was jeopardizing the quality of the cloth, and an ageing workforce as factors for review. The antidote to further decline was significant investment in machinery, marketing, cloth protection and updated processes before the Harris Tweed industry collapsed completely.

In the 1990s renewed interested from the fashion industry signalled a resurgence in tweed production, with large brands coveting the beauty of artisanal fabric. Prospective customers in the past were said to have shunned Harris Tweed because of its perceived scratchy texture and weight, so industry processes and machines were reformed with the introduction of new double-

A Mark One Hattersley loom, known as the 'workhorse' of the early Harris Tweed industry, is housed in the modern Urgha Loom Shed.

width looms and a softening of the tweed itself, which did much for the cloth's image. In 1990 John Griffiths was commissioned to build a new double-width, foot-operated loom with a bicycle-type movement. Arriving on the island in 1992, the Bonas Griffiths Rapier Handloom was larger, quieter and less labour-intensive than the Hattersley, which had come before it. The old shuttles were replaced with a rapier system which eliminated the need for pirn winding, and the outputs met the commercial demand for wider cloth. Now used by the majority of weavers working on the island, the Griffiths loom might not possess the romance of the single-width Domestic Hattersley but the high efficiency of the new loom can outweigh nostalgic longings.

THE HARRIS TWEED ACT

Harris Tweed is the only fabric in the world with its own Act of Parliament. Defining and protecting Harris Tweed was made much easier in 1993 with the introduction of the Harris Tweed Act. It dictated that every metre of fabric was to be made from pure virgin wool that was spun and dyed in the Outer Hebrides then handwoven and finished by the islanders in their homes.

The Act also created a statutory public authority, with the Harris Tweed Association becoming the Harris Tweed Authority. The authority was given the remit of: 'furthering the Harris Tweed industry as a means of livelihood for those who live in the Outer Hebrides by safeguarding the standard and reputation, promoting awareness in all parts of the world and disseminating information about material falling within the definition of Harris Tweed.'[4] Final tweed designs are now inspected by the authority and, if approved, are stamped with the orb mark to demonstrate the cloth's authenticity.

Lorna Macaulay, Chief Executive of the Harris Tweed Authority, said: 'Recognizing that the world was progressing at a fast pace, a group of people from 1989 to 1993 worked hard to get the Act of Parliament through. They had real vision to protect something that was so unique and special and important to this island economy. We are told that if we tried to push the Act through today we would struggle. At the Harris Tweed Authority our role is to promote and protect the certification mark in over fifty countries which is a fairly constant task of evidencing to trademark examiners that we are using the mark, protecting it from people who are trying to misuse or infringe it. Our trademarks are registered in two classes – cloth and pieced goods but we're looking to expand that remit because the early visionaries of Harris Tweed wouldn't have foreseen the popularity of online marketplaces that can act as a threat to our industry.'[5]

Further protection of the trademark came in 2016 when the orb was officially recognized as a coat of arms. The Lord Lyon, King of Arms agreed that the orb should become the Harris Tweed coat of arms, giving the industry further ammunition against imitation

tweeds. The coat of arms incorporates the Harris Tweed Authority mark, a motto 'guardian of the orbs' and a Gaelic phrase *Ughdarras a Chlo Hearaich* (Trustee of Harris Tweed).

A DECADE OF DEVELOPMENT 2006–2016

When Kenneth Mackenzie Ltd in Stornoway was bought in December 2006 by the experienced textile manufacturer Brian Haggas, the Harris Tweed industry found itself in flux again. The Mackenzie mill was the island's largest tweed producer and, dating back to 1906, the oldest producer of tweed in the Outer Hebrides, with a rich history of bespoke manufacturing. In a bid to streamline and modernize the business Haggas introduced a new production model to much local objection, trimming the mill's 8,500 patterns to just four to service the men's jacket market. By attempting to dominate the industry and refusing to sell tweed to outside companies and with total control of production, Haggas could make as much tweed as he needed then close down the mill mid-year to await further orders. This new model, which replaced bespoke manufacturing with off-the-peg products, proved catastrophic and after announcing waves of redundancies the mill was later forced to revert to previous production methods to survive. Often depicted as the villain in the Harris Tweed story, Haggas had a sizable hand in this period of decline, yet given the industry's pre-existing state it would be unfair to blame the entirety of its fall on one man. An unexpected and fortunate side-effect of Haggas's tight restrictions on mill outputs meant that dormant mills were revived to satisfy demand for tweed that was no longer available from the Kenneth Mackenzie mill.

In 2008, Harris Tweed Hebrides began production after oil industry executive Ian Taylor invested £2.5 million on re-equipping the Shawbost mill and resurrecting bespoke manufacturing. Led by Chief Executive Ian Angus Mackenzie and chairman Brian Wilson, Harris Tweed Hebrides is currently the largest producer of tweed on the islands. The company did not experience easy beginnings, with mill closures and general unsettlement in the industry caused by a declining and ageing workforce, and as production reached a new low it was clear that the industry needed substantial redevelopment to recover. The Harris Tweed

Bales of grey folded Harris Tweed are piled high at the Kenneth Mackenzie Mill in Stornoway.

Liaison Group subsequently commissioned research to explore the possibility of increasing sales by opening up a new market in Japan.

Despite fears that the cloth could be lost forever, Harris Tweed reached its highest level of production in almost fifteen years in 2012, a remarkable turnaround considering previous fears that the cloth could die out. More than 1 million metres/1.1 million yards of tweed were produced by the three surviving Harris Tweed mills that year, the highest level of cloth production since 1993. Even though the Outer Hebrides had been suffering from a population decline, its main export kept islanders in sustainable jobs. Most of these islanders combined weaving with keeping livestock and farming the land. In 2013 the island's third and smallest mill at Carloway announced that Chinese textile firm Shandong Ruyi had taken a shareholding in the business and had plans to export to the lucrative Chinese market. These ambitions were not fully realized and the mill, which employed twenty-seven people and provided yarn to thirty weavers, considered voluntary administration.

MODERN PRODUCTION

Harris Tweed is no longer completely handmade, with modern methods being introduced to improve efficiency. Nevertheless, the spirit of the cottage industries remains with the traditional textures and colours of the tweed remaining consistent. The cloth is still woven at the weavers' homes; however, the wool is sent to a depot to be graded and sorted. Gone are the days of weavers washing and carding the wool themselves to separate the fibres for shaping. Now the mills pack the wool into large containers and dye them - part of Harris Tweed's unique appeal is found in this dyeing process. Bales of 100 per cent pure new wool are dyed before being spun, meaning that a variety of colours can be blended before making the yarn. The wool is loaded into large stainless steel dyeing drums that force the dye into the wool using a mixture of high pressure, natural dyes and fixing chemicals. The wool is dried to remove any remaining moisture before being blended.

There are infinite colour options where tweed is concerned; typically between two and four colours are selected and measured in exact proportions before being blended together. Every mill has a specific recipe for each final colour, which requires very precise amounts of the base colours to guarantee a consistent shade of yarn. Roughly torn sections of wool are mixed together to ensure an even distribution of each colour before being shredded into a fine granular blend. The resulting light and fluffy mixture is carried through a tube to a storage space before being taken to the carding area.

The structure of the tweed comes together as the individual fibres are sorted and straightened to make yarn. Carding separates the mass mountain of blended wool into delicate threads. Once done by hand, modern

A wooden shuttle holding the pirn is thrown across the loom to carry the thread back and forth to weave the weft.

machinery now follows the same process of teasing the wool apart using metal teeth. As the wool flows through a series of machines it is continuously pulled and manipulated and becomes light in consistency ready to be made into thread by a Roving machine. Long spinning machines operate continuously to wind the thread on to long bobbins. The necessary tension required for weaving is achieved by the spinning movement that strengthens the yarn.

The warp is the lengthwise group of threads that cross with the weft to give the tweed its pattern. The cones of tweed are arranged into a specific order on a warping frame depending on the desired pattern. Some 58 metres/80 yards make a full 'piece', the industry term for one unit of full-length tweed. Once the threads have been carefully arranged in position to suit either a 'single' or 'double' width loom, they are wound on to a beam ready to be woven by independent weavers across the Hebrides.

Once the beams (warp) and bobbins (weft) of yarn are delivered to the weavers in their homes the weaver sets up the loom, changing the draft to the correct pattern, using the correct pick wheel, hand-tying on the new yarns to the tail-ends of the previous weave, to make it easier to thread on to the loom. Harris Tweed must be woven in the homes of the islanders on a non-motorized loom. Most of the looms in use are 'double-width' but 'single-width' weaving still exists, and for both the traditional foot-pedalling method remains unchanged. Most workers weave tweed in a purpose-built loom shed beside their house or croft. It can be a painstaking and physically demanding process to keep the loom pedals in a perpetual state of motion, even after years of practice. Typically a weaver can produce 100–150 metres/110–164 yards of Harris Tweed a week depending on their other crofting activities and the urgency of the commission. The cloth is pulled from their looms when complete, carefully folded in a specific way and tied in bundles ready to be returned to the mill. The fabric is collected from the weavers and taken to the mill to be finished.

The tweed is carefully mended by darners who search every bit of the cloth for imperfections, using a light table or a backlit wooden beam. Any broken or stray threads are precisely darned and mended to ensure the fabric is perfect before it is ready for washing and waulking. The tweed is washed to remove any remaining impurities and 'waulked' or wound around a rotating wheel that smooths the fabric for a softer finish. Once the fabric is pressed it can be labelled with the orb mark and a serial number. Every metre of material is recorded with the pattern, date and details of the weaver, to allow the customer to reorder the same fabric in the future.

MAINTAINING THE INDUSTRY

A fabric with such rich history and undeniable quality requires constant policing from the statutory body, the Harris Tweed Authority. It takes great care to educate

the mills and weavers continuously about the greater good of the industry as a whole and the provisions that should be made when selling the cloth to customers. The challenge for the authority is twofold: as long as the cloth is made in accordance with the Harris Tweed Act the orb stamp must be applied, yet the Harris Tweed Authority has no control over the use of the fabric by the end customer. The mills are commercial businesses that need large-scale orders from international brands to survive and subsequently pay their workers. With around 140 weavers working on the islands today these orders are essential to the flow of an island economy. The balance between maintaining the luxurious, handmade provenance of the fabric and supplying customers who use the fabric for fast-fashion is a challenging one. Lorna Macaulay said: 'We should never be on the same page as the heavily discounted market. There are dozens of cheaper machine woven tweeds available out there and we shouldn't be in that arena. We are a primary producer so we don't control what the customer does with the cloth. It's a misnomer that the Harris Tweed Authority can in some way veto how the cloth is used. We can't.'[6]

At present there are three Lewis-based mills producing Harris Tweed on the islands: Harris Tweed Hebrides in Shawbost; the Carloway Mill in Carloway; and Kenneth Mackenzie in

'Not only do I know the person who has woven the fabric, I've been to his weaving shed, I've sat at his loom and looked out of his window.' Patrick Grant

Stornoway. Although the modern market is buoyant, the future of these businesses is not certain. Each is owned and run by different enterprises which work with their own teams of self-employed weavers. Each mill differs in size, output and equipment used, has its own customer base and outlook on the industry. Essentially these are three commercially competing businesses that produce technically the same fabric but sell it at different price points and utilize different marketing strategies, yet despite their differences they are united in their quest to maintain the industry.

The existence of the mills is paramount to the survival of the independent weavers who have to ensure they have somewhere to buy their yarn and finish their cloth. The mills cooperate with professional small producers who make a quality product, acknowledging that small producers service an important part of the industry. Some customers want to buy from a weaver where they can build up a one-to-one relationship and communicate that provenance to their customers, which is the strength of the smaller producers. British menswear designer Patrick Grant said: 'We use three independent weavers – Luskentyre, Garynahine and Breanish. The quality of their product is fantastic, completely uncompromised and the supply chain is very visible. Not only do I know the person who has woven the fabric, I've been to his weaving shed, I've sat at his loom and looked out of his window. The romance of that story is invaluable to our consumer'.[7]

With its ageing workforce, Harris Tweed was in danger of disappearing but investment in the industry has allowed for training and mentoring programmes, new looms and apprenticeships in the mills to educate a new generation of weavers and mill workers. Continued investment will sustain and protect the current workforce while introducing newcomers who will produce tweed in years to come. In 2012 the European Structural Fund supported the Harris Tweed Training and Development Programme, a project based on previous training programmes with two additional New Start Weaver courses held in 2012–13. These courses were deliberately flexible to accommodate trainees who couldn't participate on a full-time basis; they largely targeted women who were under-represented in the industry. The demand for weavers is a direct result of revived interest in the fabric, particularly from fashion designers. Although not solely reliant on fashion trends, the garment industry plays a substantial part in maintaining Harris Tweed producers.

The Harris Tweed Authority is investigating labelling technology, which will allow every garment to be tagged with a corresponding code. Customers will buy a Harris Tweed garment with a unique code that can be used to access traceable content about who made the fabric, how it was woven and information about their weaving set-up, thereby fulfilling the authority's mission to share the story of a cottage industry in a contemporary way.

clockwise from top left Finished tweed for sale complete with official Harris Tweed swing tag; fashion designer Adam Skyner wears Harris Tweed waistcoat and trousers, London, 2013; cushion covers, hand-woven and hand-knitted by Joanne Owens; Harris Tweed is widely used as a jacket fabric because of its practical and durable weave.

COCO CHANEL IN SCOTLAND

Gabrielle 'Coco' Chanel modelling an early version of the tweed suit jacket in 1929.

Since their introduction in 1954, Chanel's tweed jackets have been a must-have item for the wealthy, with the bouclé tweed offering a feminine luxury feel, and a shape that blends the tailored jacket with that of a cardigan. But it was thirty years earlier, in 1924, that Gabrielle Chanel was first inspired to utilize Scottish textiles in her couture.

Chanel's fashion influence is widespread, and her ground-breaking garçonne look in the 1920s changed the way women dressed. She created clothes for the modern woman and for those who wanted to look sporty even if they didn't participate; for them she used comfortable, wearable fabrics such as jersey and tweed. It was clothing based on the masculine fashions of the men she associated with, from the aristocrats in their hunting clothes and smart tailoring to stable boys on hunting estates, who wore jodhpurs and jackets.

Chanel's attraction to Scottish fabrics was cultivated when she spent summers in the Highlands with the second Duke of Westminster in the mid-1920s. The duke, known to his friends as Bendor, was said to be Britain's wealthiest man at that time. On fishing and hunting trips to his estate in Scotland, she would slip on the duke's tweed coats and Fair Isle knits. Then she began to look to the traditional fabrics of Scotland to find her materials, visiting a local mill where she would first source pieces of rough tweed. This inspired her to introduce tweed into her fashion collections, with blazers, waistcoats, cardigans and shirts with cuff links mimicking the clothes worn by the duke and his friends.

CHANEL'S EARLY YEARS

Gabrielle Chanel had been born into poverty in 1883 in Pays de la Loire. Her early childhood was spent travelling with her mother and itinerant father, who sold ladies' underwear from town to town. Chanel was twelve years old when her mother died, and soon after her father left his three daughters in an orphanage in Aubazine, which was run by frugal and disciplined nuns.[1] Having learnt sewing over the six years spent at Aubazine, Chanel found work as a seamstress as well as a café entertainer at cabaret venues, where she earned her nickname, Coco, from the popular song 'Ko Ko Ri Ko', a play on words for 'coquette'.[2] While performing at a club in Moulin around 1903 she met a wealthy, ex-cavalry officer and polo player, Etienne Balsan, and for the next three years she stayed with him at his château Royallieu near Compiègne, where horse-racing was the premier pursuit.[3]

Through Balsan, Chanel met a wealthy young aristocrat, Boy Capel, who would be her first love and would leave her devastated when he married someone else, and again when he died in a car accident. It was Boy Capel who cemented her admiration for the style of dress of the British aristocracy, and it was he who would fund her first business ventures. Chanel's business thrived during the First World War as her fashions were

above A model wearing a pink Chanel suit in the 1960s.

above right Coco Chanel adjusting actress Romy Schneider's Chanel suit at her salon on rue Cambon, Paris in 1960.

simple and wearable for women in wartime France, with practical features such as useful pockets to replace the need for a handbag.[4] Her work always centred around masculine styles adapted into feminine designs – a tomboy fashion turned haute couture, and in the 1920s she embraced a boyish look with flapper dresses, jersey and tweed sports clothes.

Chanel first met the forty-four-year-old Duke of Westminster in Monte Carlo in late 1923, when she was in town for Christmas and new year with the Russian Grand Duke Dmitri Pavlovich. Recently separated from his second wife, Westminster was one of Europe's most eligible

'She fishes from morning to night and in two months has killed fifty salmon. She is very agreeable – really a great and strong being fit to rule a man or an empire.' Winston Churchill

bachelors and, impressed by her 'French and lively' character, he asked Chanel to dinner on his yacht, *Flying Cloud*. She subsequently spent time at the duke's vast estate, Reay Forest in remote Sutherland, surrounded by natural beauty and breathing in the crisp Highland air. They hunted, fished on the River Laxon and played cards in cosy Stack Lodge with its roaring fire and stag antlers on the walls. Chanel called it an 'absurd fairy tale', the way that Westminster's homes across Europe were always set up for arrival, with staff awaiting, bedrooms made, dinner prepared and fires lit, and, as she said, 'on the moors of Scotland, the grouse are ready to be shot, or the salmon to be fished.'[5]

Chanel biographer Justine Picardie discovered details of the three summers Chanel spent with the duke in Sutherland by going through the records of his estate and finding notes of the salmon Chanel caught. In fact, Chanel excelled at salmon fishing throughout the summer of 1925, frequently catching specimens from the River Laxon, next to the hunting lodge.[6] Winston Churchill was a regular companion at their Highland retreat, as he was a close friend of the duke, having served with him during the Boer War. In a 1927 letter to his wife Clemmie, Churchill noted: 'She fishes from morning to night and in two months has killed fifty salmon. She is very agreeable – really a great and strong being fit to rule a man or an empire.'[7]

The duke favoured Scottish tweeds for hunting and fishing, with Fair Isle jumpers worn under the jackets. This style shaped Chanel's own dress style, as she borrowed the duke's tweed jackets to keep warm and wore them with cashmere cardigans, trousers and boots. The understated, aristocratic, sporty clothes worn by the duke – from his impeccable hunting gear to his luxurious yachting wear – fired her creativity. From 1926 to 1931, her style paid tribute to the English aristocracy, from the duke's two-tone shoes to the woven, fluid jackets that were crucial to the House of Chanel.

CHANEL'S SCOTTISH TEXTILES

Chanel was also inspired by the traditions of the Highlands, particularly a handwoven woollen textile that would be the inspiration behind the iconic bouclé of the classic Chanel suit. Despite its rough quality, she sourced it from a local mill and began incorporating this fabric into her outfits and designs, in colours inspired by Scotland and its granite, moss and bracken.[8]

below left Chanel in Paris, 1929, wearing a suit inspired by the tweed jackets of English aristocracy.

below Chanel with the Duke of Westminster at Chester races in 1924. The duke introduced the designer to the Scottish Highlands and traditional fabrics.

318-KC75

left Models wear the Chanel suit on the streets of New York in a 1961 *Life* magazine editorial.

below Versions of the Chanel suit in 1977, modelled outside the salon on rue Cambon, Paris.

In the late 1920s Chanel began buying tweeds from Linton Tweeds, the Carlisle mill founded by highly regarded Scottish textile producer William Linton. Linton chose jewel tones and pastels to suit Chanel's colour palette, in fine light woollens with a bouclé surface, transforming the traditional Scottish weave into a feminine and luxurious fabric. From then on tweed would be used in every one of Chanel's collections with custom-made textures and colours that would match her specification.[9]

William Linton had been born in 1872 in Selkirk, a town built on the traditions of tweed mills since 1767. Those who grew up in the Tweed valley towns were raised on a multitude of skills such as weaving, darning and dyeing and were guaranteed jobs in the mills. Linton began working as a tweed-maker in Hawick, before taking his skills over the border to Carlisle, where he established Linton Tweeds in 1912 as a supplier for the luxury market. Linton's tweed in the 1920s was bright and fashionable, and sold to the chic Parisians of the jazz age.[10]

Chanel was introduced to Linton in 1928 by fashion designer Edward Molyneux, who was within the same wealthy European circle. Molyneux, a typically English designer and protégé of Lucile, became one of Europe's wealthy society people who spent time in Monte Carlo. When Molyneux designed Princess Marina's wedding trousseau in 1934, he specially commissioned Linton to make a tweed in a new shade of blue, inspired by azure sea, peacocks and turquoise; it would be called Marina tweed. Designer Charles Creed once said of Linton that he was 'a genius in the designing and weaving of tweeds – the greatest artist in the world, I would say, in colour combination in this material.' After William Linton's death in 1938, his daughter Agnes took over the business. She was believed to be the first woman enrolled at Galashiels' Scottish College of Textiles, and she worked closely with Chanel on the tweeds to help her relaunch her collection in 1954.[11]

26000.

John F. Kennedy with Jackie Kennedy in her iconic pink Chanel suit on the day of his assassination in Dallas in November 1963.

THE CHANEL SUIT

Chanel became one of the most prestigious designers to champion Scottish textiles, utilizing them in every collection – Fair Isle knits, tweeds, tartan and cashmere (which to this day is still created in a Scottish Borders mill, Barrie Knitwear). In July 1927 *Vogue* ran a piece on Chanel and the 'guide to chic for Scotland,' and then in October of the same year American *Vogue* named Chanel as the first designer to use tweeds as an important component of her designs. The magazine reported: 'Chanel, an important influence on modes, whose clothes are invariably simple, practical and beautiful, is making a feature of models of Scotch tweed in her recent collections. Some of these appeared in the summer, and still more are shown in her autumn collection.'[12]

In 1933, Harvey Nichols advertised a Chanel ready-to-wear sweater: 'You simply must have at least one of these jumpers . . . the latest creation of Mademoiselle Chanel but actually made in Scotland.' The first of Chanel's feminine tweed jackets were thigh length and worn with pleated skirts, while some were paired with leather, Russian-inspired belts. The loose-fitting tailored jacket would be combined with the collarless style of a cardigan – and the Chanel tweed jacket was born.

Chanel closed her business during the Second World War and fled to Switzerland to live in exile. Some fifteen years after her previous collection, she felt the time was right to make a comeback. In a sea of Dior New Look fashions, she wanted her new line to be wearable, comfortable and accessible. She again looked to Scottish tweeds for a style of suit that would be revolutionary. Chanel's first post-war collection was released on 5 February 1954, with a series of knee-length skirts and cardigan-cut jackets and skirts in soft tweeds. The suits took 150 hours of labour, using lightweight natural fabric, while a ribbon in the skirt's waistband fixed it to its blouse.

It was not immediately well received by the European press, which was hoping for something more spectacular, but American publications loved it. Chanel was celebrated by *Life* magazine, and Suzy Parker appeared on the cover of *Elle* in November 1954 wearing vermillion tweed to showcase the perfect suit for women whose busy lives meant they required adaptable clothes.

Chanel continued to develop the classic Chanel tweed suit in further collections, later with the inclusion of a blouse that matched the suit's quilted lining, to help form the structure. It would be the ultimate bourgeois suit for independent, modern women in the 1960s, and updates would include gilt chains and a bar brooch to close the jacket. The bouclé suit would forever go down in history when Jacqueline Kennedy wore a pink tweed Chanel suit and pillbox hat on the day that John F. Kennedy was assassinated in Dallas in 1963.

TWEED IN CONTEMPORARY FASHION

Contemporary tweed fashions for both men and women, as shown in Walker Slater's spring 2016 collection.

A regular on international catwalks, tweed is no longer an old-fashioned fabric reserved for hunting and fishing. Contemporary designers have fuelled its popularity with modern accessories sold alongside the familiar tweed sporting jacket, allowing contemporary and traditional design to coexist. High-fashion houses such as Prada, Erdem, Hugo Boss, Christian Dior, Chanel and Louis Vuitton have all sent vibrant tweed down the catwalk.

Although they manipulate the fabric to suit modern trends, the cloth retains its heritage, with the demand for daring colours and patterns evolving alongside subtle greens, browns, purples and blues reminiscent of the Scottish landscape where they are woven. Having weathered moments of uncertainty, Harris Tweed has become one of the fashion industry's most desired fabrics as a new wave of contemporary designers explore the versatility of the cloth.

TWEED VISIONARIES

Chanel

Chanel's love affair with tweed, which began back in 1924 when the fashion house's eponymous founder Gabrielle 'Coco' Chanel was holidaying in the Scottish Highlands (see page 132), was continued by Karl Lagerfeld when he was appointed Artistic Director at the company in 1982, after several changes in leadership following Coco Chanel's death in 1971.

Lagerfeld was tasked with restoring an ailing fashion house to its former grandeur. His first collection in 1983 was met with critical acclaim, referencing Coco's collections from the 1920s and 1930s in favourites like the little black dress, panelled jackets and of course luxurious tweeds with vibrant multicoloured checks. Lagerfeld has continued to reinvent the classic fabric using shots of metallic, pops of colour and inserts of denim and leather, nodding to the principle of versatility that Chanel herself championed. Lagerfeld said: 'Absolute respect would have been fatal to creativity, I took the Chanel codes, or language and I mixed them up. Mademoiselle's basic idea was timeless modernity. But my job was primarily to reinvent Chanel. So I played with the codes, manipulated them, sometimes even eliminated them before bringing them back.'[1]

Tweed was a consistent feature of Coco's collections and Lagerfeld purposely maintained the relationship with Carlisle-based mill Linton Tweeds when he joined the fashion house, focusing his attentions on the tweed skirt suit that had been so popular throughout the 1980s and 1990s. For each collection the tweed mill weaves up to a dozen exclusive fabric samples for Lagerfeld who will choose two or three favourites to be produced and subsequently made into prototype garments. Chairman of Linton Tweeds Leslie Walker remembers: 'Karl Lagerfeld would send his inspirational ideas, often in the form of abstract paintings, a colour picture, a photograph of a vineyard or other artefacts, asking for fabric to be designed to capture the essence of the

'Karl Lagerfeld would send his inspirational ideas, often in the form of abstract paintings, a colour picture . . . or other artefacts, asking for fabric to be designed to capture the essence of the picture.' Leslie Walker of Linton Tweeds

Claudia Schiffer in a black tweed Chanel suit embroidered with a white and black braid, designed by Karl Lagerfeld for the spring/summer collection, Paris, 1995.

picture, with colours and textures being all important to a faithful interpretation of his muse.'[2]

Lagerfeld's tweed has been mixed with silk, linen, cotton and even rubber to realize new iterations of Chanel's signature two-piece. Keeping the original Chanel archive at the heart of his work, Lagerfeld hired a group of young models to wear the reinvented skirt suit thus inspiring a new generation of tastemakers – from Claudia Schiffer in the 1990s in her tweed jacket and leather miniskirt during the age of the supermodel, with Linda Evangelista, Naomi Campbell and Schiffer leading the trend for bare skin, bra-tops and miniskirts, to Kendall Jenner and Gigi Hadid in 2015 with their colourful cropped blazers. His re-imagined traditional tweed, now made in Paris by the House of Lesage, is coveted by a younger customer snapping up the classic Chanel tweed jacket to wear with ripped jeans or denim shorts.

Lagerfeld had never shown a Chanel tweed for men until his autumn 2004 collection, where he sent out male models in a garçon-inspired suit, but masculine design details do exist throughout his women's collections, most notably inspired by Coco's love life. In March 2005 *Vogue* reported that the autumn/winter collection had tweed plus fours inspired by the ones Coco herself used to wear in the days of her relationship with the Duke of Westminster.[3] In December 2008 Lagerfeld's annual Métiers d'Art show celebrated Coco's connection with Russian émigrés in Paris with tweeds appearing in a white snow-queen ensemble

below left Kate Moss for Chanel, Paris, 1995.

below right Chanel autumn/winter 2012/2013 collection at the Grand Palais, Paris Fashion Week.

and red skirt suit. Later in January 2009 in a show held at rue Cambon, white tweed jackets were worn with A-line skirts. In a Chanel video titled 'The Jacket' Karl Lagerfeld said: 'The Chanel jacket is a man's jacket that has become typically feminine which has definitely come to symbolize a certain nonchalant feminine elegance that is timeless.'[4]

The fashionable status of tweed reached a new high in 2012 when Lagerfeld held the Métiers d'Art fashion show in Scotland. Metres of tartan and tweed were given a couture reinvention, worn by Cara Delevingne, Stella Tennant and Edie Campbell amid the ruins of fifteenth-century Linlithgow Palace, the birthplace of Mary Queen of Scots. The models were wrapped in textured sweaters from Barrie Knitwear, a Scottish Borders mill bought by Chanel after its owner went into administration, layered over tartan skirts and dresses that served their purpose of showcasing local craftsmanship.

An advocate of innovation, Lagerfeld once said: 'Energy should always be new. There is no old energy. You cannot stock energy. You can for electricity but not for creativity'.[5] With experimentation in mind Lagerfeld continues to develop new textiles showing a laser-cut leather suit in autumn 2015 with a grid pattern that mimicked a classic tweed design. Nodding to past Chanel traditions while retaining a contemporary aesthetic is how Lagerfeld's reinvention of tweed, a traditional Chanel motif, has helped to secure the fashion house's future.

Alexander McQueen

With an admiration for heritage and ancestry and a love of nature, McQueen's kinship with Scotland and his affinity with the country's history and fabrics presented itself in complex ways. Contrasts of darkness and light filled his work and for McQueen it seemed that fashion was not just a means of self-expression but also a vehicle that allowed him to plunge the viewer into his dramatic world where witchcraft and violence coexisted with nostalgia and gentle sensitivity.

His design philosophy to 'make a piece that can transcend any trend and will still hold as much presence in 100 years time'[6] was evident in Widows of Culloden (2006), a refined collection that benefited from the skills McQueen had developed during his time as chief designer of womenswear at Givenchy (1996–2001). Despite his well-documented difficulties at the refined French fashion house he admitted: 'I learned lightness at Givenchy. At Givenchy I learned to soften. Working at Givenchy helped me learn my craft.'[7]

Inspired by the Jacobite Risings that culminated in the Battle of Culloden (1746), Widows of Culloden was a memorial to the women who were left behind. Invites branded with a black and white cameo of an Edwardian girl with the Gaelic title '*Bantraich de cuil lodair*' gave guests little clue about the theatrical show that was to come. Models walked along a square catwalk of rough wooden boards around a central glass pyramid to a mixed soundtrack of Scottish bagpipes overlaid with

clockwise from left Alexander McQueen at Paris Fashion Week: tweed skirt and jacket, autumn/winter 2006/2007; Hitchcock-inspired collection for autumn/winter 2005/2006; tweed suit with feather headpiece by Philip Treacy, autumn/winter 2006/2007.

drums and howling Highland winds wearing a series of elegantly tailored tweeds mirroring the aristocratic image of McQueen's muse Isabella Blow.

The collection was presented in three vast explorations of peasant and upper-class dress beginning with mixed neutral tweeds and feathers followed by MacQueen tartan and leather. He finished with regal black gowns and an exquisite ivory tulle and lace dress with antique lace veil that had been fractured by a headpiece of resin antlers. Ever at the forefront of his mind, ornithology and gamekeeping were prominent with feathery plumes rising from a series of bird's-nest headdresses created by McQueen's long-time collaborator Philip Treacy and decorated with speckled blue topaz and smoky quartz Swarovski crystals by jeweller Shaun Leane to accessorize the beautifully fitted tweed suits and coats. McQueen's collaborative team was central to the success of his shows with 'hours of beading and labour in every catwalk piece passed through many skilled hands.'[8]

The haunting yet ethereal 'Pepper's Ghost' installation of Kate Moss within a large glass pyramid wearing a silk organza dress and moving to the eerie soundtrack of *Schindler's List* (1993) epitomized McQueen's fascination with death and marked the dramatic finale to Widows of Culloden. The optical illusion would later complete *Savage Beauty*, the largest retrospective of the designer's work presented in Europe held at the Victoria & Albert Museum. With more than 200 pieces on display, the exhibition captured the theatre synonymous with McQueen's dramatic catwalk shows and allowed the general public to explore McQueen's creative mind. Originally presented at The Costume Institute of the Metropolitan Museum of Art in New York, it was the V&A's most successful exhibition with more than 480,000 tickets sold.[9]

Widows of Culloden's elaborate and stately image was a far cry from McQueen's macabre, vitriolic dedication to Scotland seen almost eleven years earlier. Arguably his most controversial, McQueen's fourth show, Highland Rape, was intended as a statement on the suffering of his Scottish ancestors (see page 95). He was also inspired by Patrick Suskind's novel *Perfume: The Story of a Murderer,* where virgins are brutally killed in the protagonist's search for the ultimate scent. Criticized for going to extremes to communicate a vision, McQueen was accused of objectifying women and glamorizing sexual violence. The critics were largely in agreement

A model wears a signature structured jacket and fitted pencil skirt by Vivienne Westwood, Paris Fashion Week autumn/winter 1995.

however that McQueen's unique talent for tailoring and his manipulation of budget materials was exquisite despite the extreme darkness of the subject matter.

In the years that followed McQueen's aesthetic softened, his clothes became more commercial and the signature show-time theatrics were less prevalent. His figure-hugging, waist-cinching tweed suits for the Hitchcock-inspired autumn/winter 2005 show titled 'The Man Who Knew Too Much' flashed the feminine form, but this was 1960s' glamour not chest-baring and bumsters. While some critics wondered if McQueen was playing it safe, his penchant for provocation appeared in the shattered glass catwalk and garments of Horn of Plenty (autumn/winter 2009/2010). Amid a set dressed with a heap of all-black rubbish including mechanical parts and props from his previous shows, McQueen parodied Christian Dior houndstooth suits and Chanel tweed to communicate his frustration with commercial fashion consumption at a time when the economy was in a state of flux.

Vivienne Westwood

More than any other contemporary designer, Vivienne Westwood has consistently chosen tweed to bring her fashionable creations to life, using the fabric to reinvent periods in history and dated perceptions of woven textiles. She reinvented tweed and British tailoring traditions for another generation in her historical and punk-inspired Harris Tweed collection.

After a period of being out of fashion, tweed experienced a revival, embraced by British mod culture in the 1960s and 1970s and revived by Westwood in 1987 when she returned to London Fashion Week after a five-year absence with her autumn/winter Harris Tweed collection. Fine tuning the ideas she explored in Mini-Crini, Westwood's Harris Tweed collection represented 'the ebullience of punk segued into the swagger of fine tailoring with lush references to the past.'[10] Exploring British tradition with Savile Row-inspired tailored jackets that parodied the upper-class gentry, she was inspired by memories of the clothes worn by young Princesses Margaret and Elizabeth and the collection marked her avid interest in British heritage and a growing obsession with the Establishment. It also revealed a significant change in her design aesthetic with a focus on very fitted, highly tailored separates. In an interview with *i-D* magazine Westwood said: 'My whole idea for this collection was stolen from a little girl I saw on the tube one day. She wouldn't have been more than fourteen. She had a little plaited bun, a Harris Tweed jacket and a bag with a pair of ballet shoes in it. She looked so cool and composed, standing there. Everyone around her was being noisy and rowdy, but she looked quite serene'.[11]

Despite the complexity of its design, Westwood's Harris Tweed collection was reportedly pulled together on a shoestring budget in her London flat

on her original sewing machine. Many key pieces from the collection, including the tailored 'Statue of Liberty' corset, based on the reinvention of an eighteenth-century design, and the 'Savile' jackets, became Westwood classics, while the memory of Sadie Frost in a Harris Tweed coat and cap over a ballet-style, blue satin corset and tulle skirt secured a cult following for tweed fabric itself. Later Westwood would adapt the Harris Tweed symbol to create her own logo featuring an orb with a cross surrounded by the rings of Saturn.

In the following years from 1988–90 her collections fell under the title Britain Must Go Pagan. Most notable in this period was the 1988 Time Machine collection named after the H.G. Wells novel, where Westwood refined her use of Harris Tweed with precisely tailored suits and structured jackets inspired by medieval armour. The unusual bands of tweed running around the waistline of a Breanish tweed jacket kept the fabric close to the body and were based on the Norfolk sporting jacket worn from the mid-1870s to the 1920s.

Subsequent collections would feature tweed heavily, from the standout striped skirt suit in Breanish Tweed for Portrait (autumn/winter 1990/1991) with its short, double-breasted jacket fastened with oversized amber buttons, to the double-breasted power jackets of On Liberty (autumn/winter 1994/1995). This featured a feminine hourglass shape of padded hips and shoulders and nipped waist, using yellow and brown Harris Tweed and adding a cushion bustle to the rear that was inspired by late nineteenth-century silhouettes.

From the moment *Women's Wear Daily*'s John Fairchild listed Westwood alongside Yves Saint Laurent, Giorgio Armani, Emmanuel Ungaro, Karl Lagerfeld and Christian Lacroix as one of the 'top six designers in the world' in 1989, her reputation as a fashion maverick was cemented. When Westwood began her fashion career in 1970 she would not have envisioned such critical acclaim, particularly considering her recurring themes

clockwise from top Dashing Tweeds' Mayfair Store at 26 Sackville Street, London; a herringbone tweed waistcoat and trousers by Scottish tweed specialists Walker Slater, spring 2016; coordinating long and short Harris Tweed waistcoats by Elizabeth Martin.

of subverting the Establishment and a penchant for eccentricity. Despite being known for basing much of her work within the realm of historical excess, Vivienne Westwood is cited as one of the twentieth century's most forward-thinking fashion visionaries, continuing to reinvent classic tailoring and manipulate the native British fabrics she has so consistently used throughout her career.

CONTEMPORARY TWEED

Reinventing tweed for a demanding contemporary consumer is a difficult task, but in the hands of the experts a perfect balance between history, heritage and modern fashion is achievable. From the oldest bespoke tailoring firm in Scotland - Stewart Christie and Co – to Savile Row and British fashion designers Nigel Cabourn and Margaret Howell, a collective of industry leaders are intelligently selling relevant, practical and fashionable tweed.

Developing a new tweed pattern typically begins with a source of textural inspiration. Menswear designer Patrick Grant said: 'Once it was a photograph of a peeling concrete wall at a football stadium in the north of England in the 1950s. We took that and created a jacquard tweed based on an abstraction of that pattern. For another collection it was the wallpaper on the inside of a crofter's cottage. From there we pick yarn colours and work backwards and forwards with the weavers'.[12] Experimenting with cityscapes is a catalyst for Savile Row newcomers Dashing Tweeds who sent images of pavements and tarmac to have matching yarns dyed that spoke of industrialism, in a bid to move tweed from the countryside into urban sportswear. Founder Guy Hills is a former photographer and was inspired by the richness and colour that men once had in their wardrobes. He introduced the idea of urban tweeds by merging the different shapes and cuts of traditional tailoring with vibrant tweed woven in-house on a hand loom.

His contemporary tailored menswear casts woollen fabrics in a new light and moves away from the traditional Savile Row aesthetic with a clear focus on innovation, having identified that wearing tweed allowed men to experiment with colour. While this new breed of tweed has a loyal following, the company happily accommodates traditionalists searching for the rough heavy cloth, with Germans and Northern Europeans typically preferring a scratchy, heavy tweed.[13]

Their Lumatwill range involves fine 3M retro-reflective yarn being woven into the tweed. The yarn features micro glass beads that are adhered to a technical fabric base, making the fabric glow in the dark, attracting city cyclists with its luminous quality. With travel and adventure in mind, the tweed's hardwearing and functional quality is accentuated with practical button fastenings and zipped pockets. A quilted tweed waistcoat with inside pockets to hold a newspaper, earphone tabs and a phone pocket inside the gilet cater entirely to the modern man.

For their autumn/winter 2016 collection, Dashing Tweeds worked with Dundee firm Haley Stevenson on a dry wax finish, which made the tweed totally waterproof. The resulting garment – described as 'a cross between a motorbike jacket and a quilted waterproof jacket'[14] – saw tweed become a performance fabric. In the future the company hopes to use fibres that can connect pockets with Bluetooth using nanotechnology. According to Hills: 'There will be a time when screens are part of clothes and integration is closer to the body. The worlds of tech and tradition can co-exist where the construction of clothes is relevant for the everyday lifestyle.'[15]

Dashing Tweeds can be seen as 'hi-tech London estate tweeds'[16] transcending social classes and following a very particular form and function. Its vibrant cloth has been used by Savile Row firm Norton & Sons, which has collaborated with young British designers including Giles Deacon, Richard Nicoll and Christopher Kane. Norton & Sons tailored the purple Argyll Dashing Tweed worn by Agyness Deyn for House of Holland's autumn/winter 2008/2009 show, keeping its well-established brand relevant in an ever-changing marketplace, 'challenging cutters to incorporate Edwardian millinery, safari and court tailoring techniques into contemporary fashion tailoring'.[17]

Relevance is paramount in the fashion sphere where the heritage fibre has to be practical and useful to a modern audience. Rather than competing with mass-market mills, Hills concentrates on quality and clever

left, above and below Fisher tweed design by Dashing Tweeds in navy wool with alternating yellow and red chevroned stripes; a Dashing Tweeds design in Shetland wool with block checks inspired by the work of 1930s Bauhaus weaver Gunta Stölzl.

marketing: 'There are varying levels of luxury but educated people typically buy luxury that has real depth. Genuine cloth is a luxury item with years of skill and experience in it. Sweat shops are unsustainable and eventually everyone will realize that good quality costs money.'[18]

Fellow arbiter of quality is designer Nigel Cabourn, known for his practical, hardy menswear and often favouring rough and raw tweed that withstands the elements and the rigours of time. A tweed advocate since 1973, Cabourn describes 1970s' tweed as 'rough, coarse and heavy, produced on Hattersley looms in narrow widths and only available in a standard weight of 560–590 grams'.[19]

His classic 'Mallory' Harris Tweed jacket (from his 2003 Ascent of Cabourn collection) is named after George Mallory whose body was recovered from the slopes of Everest seventy-five years after his fatal attempt to reach the top. According to Cabourn around 1,000 Mallory jackets are sold a year, and the most popular are in lightweight army green, black or navy Harris Tweed.

Inspired by explorers, adventure and an extensive personal archive of historical memorabilia, Cabourn prefers to 'adapt and manipulate the tweed to create something new – sometimes using it raw, straight off the loom when it's not brushed or finished or tweed that's double brushed on both sides to make it look vintage'.[20]

The British designer's long-term knowledge of Harris Tweed has helped him develop tweed with new commercial finishes that lend themselves well to the demands of the modern wardrobe: 'We developed a highly practical finish by coating the tweed with dry wax. If you saturate Harris Tweed in oil it completely kills it so we used a special dry wax which makes the tweed water repellent and stiffer without ruining the feel of the fabric.'[21]

Similarly British fashion designer Margaret Howell has used the fabric extensively in her collections and is attracted by its natural colour palette. With a focus on modern classics that last a lifetime, Howell was inspired to create her own label by the discovery of a vintage man's shirt, and subsequently produced signature shirts and unstructured tweed jackets. Inspired by natural materials, Howell is passionate about landscape, and its connection with such fabrics and the skilled people who weave them. Howell's workwear aesthetic is matched with the quintessential British feeling of tweed suits in a neutral palette of navy, cream and black. Howell's longstanding kinship with tweed is to the 'depth and complexity of texture that can't be imitated by a mechanical process. The resilient wool, the designs in earthy colours – reflect the landscape, the climate and the skills of the local people who produce it.'[22] Howell explains: 'I've lived a life close to the natural landscape and love textures and colours that reflect what I see in the outdoors. Tweed has such a loftiness about it. There is life to be found in those plain weaves and little dogtooths. Customers always respond well to brown herringbone, dark grey and black but our challenge

clockwise from top left A signature black Harris Tweed frock coat by Judy R Clark; tweed suit on the streets of New York during fashion week, 2016; fitted brown tweed waistcoat and pencil skirt by Joyce Paton; brown tweed jacket complete with folded pocket square.

is to find something fresh whilst using my favourite traditional colours.'[23]

For young Scottish designer Judy R Clark the affinity with Harris Tweed is generational, linked to her uncle who weaves tweed and to her aunt who works in a tweed finishing room. Citing its 'unique quality, distinctive colourways, patterns and durability',[24] Clark uses lightweight tweeds that are popular in womenswear and eschews the days of a heavy itchy cloth that was associated with crofting life. Building on the depth of the fabric, Clark adds vintage lace, silks and velvets to the tweed, designing signature frock coats and jackets with appliquéd collars, lace cuffs and feather details. Clark trained at Alexander McQueen's London design house and subsequently set up her own label. 'Working at McQueen was an education in fabrics, design and how to run a successful fashion business. It was an honour if McQueen chose your pieces as the starting blocks to forge new ideas. I spent two weeks making colourful hand-cut and dyed silk flowers. He came into the room and cut them all with scissors to sprinkle them between the layers of a nude net dress.'[25]

TWEED FOOTWEAR

Tweed has become a regular feature in both high street and designer fashion collections with popular designs filtering from international catwalks through to high street collections. The cloth has never been more accessible and the footwear industry in particular has harnessed its widespread appeal with several multinational brands using tweed to create limited edition collections. When these brands respect the provenance of tweed and its unique qualities while introducing new processes and finishes that keep the industry moving forward, then there is room for contemporary footwear collections that appeal to a mass audience.

Nike's well-known collection of Harris Tweed and leather trainers indicated a shift in tweed's associations with traditional upper-class country sportswear by moving the cloth into the realm of modern streetwear. When a Nike designer contacted weaver Donald John Mackay in 2004, the Harris Tweed industry was in turmoil and the lifeline of a large order did much to revive the local economy. Nike was planning to feature Harris Tweed as a key part of a new Terminator trainer design, and Mackay tasked a large collective of fellow weavers across the Outer Hebrides to help fulfil the brand's order of nearly 10,000 metres/10,900 yards of cloth. Later, the launch of the Air Royalty Harris Tweed trainer in 2010 marked the second collaboration between Nike and Harris Tweed.

Other footwear brands followed suit including Converse, which created a Harris Tweed x Chuck Taylor All Star trainer, and later collaborated with Dashing Tweeds using its Regents Park check fabric. Drawing on both the cloth's quality as a handmade British product and the brand's punk heritage, Doc Martens created a range of Harris Tweed shoes as part of its Made in England range.

TWEED IN FASHION CULTURES

Paris designer Jacques Heim's 1963 teepee-style hooded cape in houndstooth check.

below Amber Anderson, Eden Clark, Erin O'Connor and Eleanor Weedon at the Rugby Ralph Lauren Tweed Run in London, 2011.

right Fashionable men's tweed suits for the city showcased in London's *West End Gazette*, July 1873.

When Ben Affleck wore a Harris Tweed jacket as a CIA man in the 2012 film *Argo*, it was revealed that this was the uniform for US spies throughout the Cold War. Production crew on *Argo* spoke to the real-life spy Tony Mendez, to ask him what he wore during his covert trip to Iran. He told them it was a Harris Tweed jacket and slacks, with Harris Tweed acting as a subtle means of indicating their work in covert international operations against Russia. 'That was our uniform,' Mendez told *The Guardian*. 'The jackets were representative of our group. Those of us in the CIA who did overseas work, work in the field. If you were in the field during the Blitz, you wore a trench coat. If you were tracking Ivan [the Soviet Union and its allies] you had Harris Tweed.'[1]

So what was it about Harris Tweed that made it the CIA choice of fashion? It's a jacket unobtrusive enough not to attract attention, it has sedate connotations as the clothing of Oxford deans, but it also indicates a certain individual flair.

With its sense of uniform formality as well as the opportunity for different colour and texture combinations, tweed lends itself to being distinct. It came to represent the dandy, Ivy League style and the mod. It traversed the wardrobe of aristocrats spending their weekends taking part in country pursuits such as hunting and shooting, as well as those of teachers and professors with their obligatory elbow patches. In the last decade tweed has become an ironic statement worn by steampunks and hipsters.

Following tweed's integration back into fashion, it has reached another peak in popularity. Harris Tweed is the trendiest of them all, finding its way into catwalk shows and as interior decoration for boutique hotels such as Blythswood Square in Glasgow, where curtains, upholstery and cushions are all in Harris Tweed, creating a cosmopolitan twist on the country fabric.

'The jackets were representative of our group. If you were in the field during the Blitz, you wore a trench coat. If you were tracking Ivan you had Harris Tweed.' CIA officer Tony Mendez

While Harris Tweed's history is of a practical fabric produced by Scottish crofters in the Outer Hebrides, it was Scots such as Sir Walter Scott who in the 1830s influenced a fashion for gentlemen to wear tweed trousers and shooting jackets. As a warm, hardy fabric it was ideal for outdoor sportswear. As has been seen earlier in this book, it was also the work of the influential Catherine Murray, Lady Dunmore, who brought Harris Tweed from the Outer Hebrides to the salons of London. 'Harris tweed was a cottage tweed, and Lady Dunmore saw it as a way of crofters being able to make money, so she took it off the island and showed it to friends, and marketed it to places like Liberty of London. She had a circle of influential friends, and so was the ideal person to get the industry going. She thought she would give it a chance and succeeded with it,' commented Anne Dunmore, the current Countess of Dunmore.[2]

A CYCLING REVOLUTION

With the advent of the bicycle, a fantastic new mode of transport that allowed men, and women, to travel around independently, tweed was used to create fashionable cyclewear.

Cycling became a craze for women in the 1890s, as they could independently travel the streets without the need for a carriage, a horse or a male companion. However, one concern was finding practical women's cycling clothes, particularly as the fashions at that time were for frills and froth. The cycling woman of the 1890s therefore chose tweed instead of silks and lace, and on the cover of Ella Hepworth Dixon's *The Story of a Modern Woman*, written in 1894, is a photograph of a female cyclist with tweed jacket and bloomers.

Comfortable sports clothes were further pushed by the Rational Dress Society, a feminist movement founded in the 1880s to promote practical clothes for women, with a recommended maximum weight for clothing of 3.2 kilograms/7 pounds. Contemporary fashion with its bustles and corsets 'impedes the movement of the body' to make 'healthy exercise almost impossible,' the Rational Dress Society wrote in the introduction to its gazette.[3]

An outdoor outfit consisting of a fitted tweed jacket and skirt had become fashionable daywear for women by the 1890s, particularly with the founding of ladies' clubs for cricket, golf and hockey. Meanwhile long tweed trousers could be worn under skirts, allowing for ease of movement when taking part in outdoor sports such as riding.

Golfer May Hezlet, who won her first British Ladies Amateur title in 1899, described her ideal outfit as a tweed skirt 15 centimetres/6 inches off the ground, with a coat to match, or a woollen or silk jersey, and a pair of good shoes with square heels.[4] There were criticisms of this type of clothing for women as tweed jackets and caps were considered mannish. *Punch* magazine suggested it was more charming for women to appear in 'ribbons and laces', and 'feminine graces', by critiquing in a rhyme: 'With garments for walking, and tennis, and talking, All terribly manful and too trouseresque/And habits for riding, for skating, or sliding/With 'rational' features they claim to possess . . .'[5]

While tweed was seen as too masculine and brusque for women, it would gain another famous Victorian depiction – and one that would influence the steampunk subculture more than 100 years later. Sir Arthur Conan Doyle's fictional detective Sherlock Holmes became known for wearing tweed after etchings by Sidney Paget appeared alongside Doyle's stories in the *Strand*, a Victorian magazine. Paget, an artist based in Finchley, produced more than 200 illustrations of Sherlock Holmes between 1891 and 1893, and a further 155 between 1901 and 1904, with Holmes dressed in a deerstalker cap and Inverness cape.[6] The tweed cape and cap became an integral part of the character's depiction in film and television, although Benedict Cumberbatch's modern incarnation of Holmes wears a Belstaff Milford coat – first made in the 1920s and inspired by a nineteenth-century heavy tweed coat.

By 1901 tweed had become such a popular fabric that there was even a tuberculosis scare in London, believed to be carried in the fibres of jackets made from Harris Tweed. According to the *New York Times* the tweed was: 'largely worn in men's sporting clothes and rough wear suits generally, which is made in little, ill-ventilated, single-room cabins by peasants among whom consumption prevails. It is believed that the cloth sent from these huts is full of whatever bacteria are generated or developed in them.'[7]

After the First World War, with clothes offering more freedom for women, and a relaxed sportswear look for men becoming increasingly common, tweed became widespread in male and female fashion. A tweed jacket was useful for motoring, while tweed plus fours were

below Three Victorian English women in tweed jackets and skirts for cycling, 1896.

right A tweed ladies' golfing outfit designed by Frederick Bosworth in 1908 and worn by Heather Firbank.

clockwise from top left Two Oxford university students in tweed jackets and 'Oxford bags' trousers enjoying a cigarette, 1925; a Norfolk jacket, dating from between 1890 and 1900, developed from the uniform of the Rifle Corps into a shooting costume in the 1860s, before becoming a versatile item for country wear; preppy Ivy League fashions in the 1950s with tweed jackets and caps the height of campus fashion.

perfect for keeping warm on the golf course. The 1920s was the era of the dandy, with sports casual and dandy fashions at universities. The Duke of Windsor, at that time the most fashionable man on the planet, made tweeds a must-have, while also representing the foppish masculinity of the jazz age. As has been explored in earlier chapters, Coco Chanel also championed tweed as a comfortable, practical yet stylish cloth for women.

THE IVY LEAGUE

American men typically dressed in a more casual way than their British counterparts, and on the university campuses they combined this sporty style with British tailoring, as London, particularly on Savile Row, was considered the centre of excellence for tailoring. To reflect this very British style, manufacturers such as Brooks Brothers purchased Scottish- and English-made tweeds, with Harris Tweed a particular favourite.[8]

Apparel Arts, a guide to dressing for young American college students, launched in 1931. The March 1937 edition noted the college man spent 51 per cent more on clothes than the 'average man', and Princeton University was the leader when it came to sartorial tips. A freshman would arrive at Princeton and soon learn how to set style trends for the whole country, with a tweed jacket as an essential item for the dress-down sporty look, worn with button-down shirts. Throughout the 1950s, this Ivy League style would also be worn on Wall Street, Madison Avenue and by modern jazz musicians such as Miles Davis and Charlie Parker. The shops on campus would be the place to buy these essentials – Harris Tweed, Madras sports jackets, seersuckers, grey flannel suits and Shetland jumpers.[9]

British mods, originally a group of jazz fans who frequented the Flamingo club in London's Soho, were inspired by Miles Davis to adopt Ivy League style mixed with Italian tailoring. As mod fashion swept the country, the houndstooth check was used to create zippy jackets and skirts for its black-and-white geometric design, which suited modernist, Op Art sentiment.

With punk, skinhead and glam-rock subcultures taking over fashion in the 1970s, designers such as Tommy Hilfiger and Ralph Lauren offered a clean Ivy League alternative with their wholesome, all-American, preppy style of ties, tweeds and chinos.

TWEED FOR SLOANE RANGERS

At the start of the 1980s, as the economy in Britain was making a recovery, a new style tribe that celebrated an aspirational way of life gathered around Fulham and Sloane Square.[10] In an update of the Mitford sisters' U and Non-U lists, these Sloane Rangers (as they were nicknamed) were upper-class men and women from the country, bringing to the city fashions such as tweed coats and skirts, wellies, body-warmers, lamb's wool sweaters and pearls. Following ITV's production of *Brideshead Revisited* in 1981 and the marriage of Prince Charles and Lady Diana Spencer, nostalgia was in the air for

below left Sloane Rangers in 1981, a group known for bringing wealthy country fashions to the city.

below Madonna with Guy Ritchie in 2004, a time when she adopted tweed fashions and moved to the English countryside.

an upper-class lifestyle, now seemingly in reach of the middle classes. Sloanes were regular visitors to Annabel's nightclub or Ménage à Trois for an Iron Lady cocktail, and shopped at Harvey Nichols, Harrods (or 'Rods) and Peter Jones department store.

In 1982, the *Official Sloane Ranger Handbook* by Peter York and Ann Barr became a bestseller as it captured the aspirational mood of the time. The handbook identified the typical Sloane Ranger as 'Caroline', or 'Henry', and this was picked up by the *New York Times* in its profile piece on the Sloane in 1984: 'Henry will be wearing a bespoke suit, dotted tie and silk handkerchief (probably also spotted). Or, perhaps, he will sport his casual garb: jeans, decent tweed jacket and either a navy Guernsey or olive army sweater; sometimes he will brighten the outfit with a yellow pullover.'[11]

The style of these 'Hooray Henrys' would influence a new public-schoolboy fashion, with fashion editor Suzy Menkes writing in *The Times* in 1982 of a menswear trend for tweed, worn with striped ties, braces and waistcoats: 'Tweed, and especially the overgrown school coat, is one of the strongest threads in the public school style . . . Margaret Howell, whose quiet English style tunes in delicately to the current look, has also made a tweed greatcoat that looks as though it belongs on a peg in the gunroom of some draughty country house.'[12]

In the mid-1980s, the preppy fashion for gentlemen in tweeds continued as the economy boomed. A group calling themselves the Young Fogeys wore their tweeds with Viyella shirts, knitted ties, V-necked sweaters and waistcoats. The new Savile Row tailors such as David Chambers created bespoke tweeds for Bryan Ferry and David Bowie, while Tommy Nutter was known for his loud tweed suits that referenced the Duke of Windsor and were worn with herringbone tweed trousers and dandyish brocade waistcoats. Marks & Spencer reported in 1985 that their Harris Tweed jackets were bestsellers, while herringbone tailoring was one of the hot trends at Harrods.[13]

However, by 1990 the popularity of tweed crashed with the stock market – as gentleman tailoring became a fragment of the 1980s in the face of grunge and acid house. Yet, a decade later, London had positioned itself as a city for billionaires, with sky-rocketing real estate in Knightsbridge and Mayfair, and Russian oligarchs and Saudis outpricing London bankers. After marrying film director Guy Ritchie in 2000, Madonna reinvented herself as lady of the manor, and she moved to a Georgian mansion in Wiltshire and took up horse riding and clay pigeon shooting. She threw herself into the English country lifestyle to suit her husband, known for his preference for all things British and for sporting a tweed cap and Barbour jacket. It was reported that: 'She bought suitable clothes, including a tweed hunting vest, moleskin trousers, a £975 cashmere field coat, knee-length breeches and a £65 cashmere shooting cap. She is the perfect hostess at their shooting parties, attended by

Participants in the annual Tweed Run in London, 2016.

showbiz friends who call her simply M – among them Brad Pitt, Sting, Vinnie Jones and chef Marco Pierre White.'[14]

By 2010, Kate Middleton had heralded a new generation of Sloane Ranger, with her casual wardrobe of tweed skirts, jackets and jeans, and her glossy mane of hair. With the influence of *Made in Chelsea*, combined with the new money excess of *The Only Way Is Essex*, fashion was once again about showcasing wealth and making upper-class statements. According to *Tatler* in 2013, the East End 'has the fastest growing Sloane tribe'.[15]

Popular British label Jack Wills referenced old British gentry and, as part of the millennial hipster movement, tweed returned as pastiche on the streets of Shoreditch. A neo-Victorian fashion for tweeds, waistcoats, brogues and beards was a way to look nostalgically to the past at a time of economic hardship and terror threats. It seemed that people looked for a notion of comfort in the face of adversity, and with this nostalgic way of dress was a desire for locally sourced, organic foods and environmental-consciousness. Because tweed was the ultimate long-lasting fabric (the Duke of Windsor boasted that he still wore a tweed jacket owned by his grandfather from the 1890s), it was a good choice for those interested in recycling clothes by wearing vintage or highly durable fabrics.

Similarly steampunks took up tweeds worn in a Victorian style but with a futuristic twist. The 'dress-up' fantasy subculture was inspired by Victorian science fiction writers such as H.G. Wells and Jules Verne, and tweed jackets, with their links to Sherlock Holmes and Victorian gentlemen, became part of the costume.[16] Vivienne Westwood was actually the first designer with a steampunk vision when she launched her Time Machine collection in 1988, combining tweed with corsetry, following the designer's rich tradition of plundering eighteenth-century fashion and British fabrics.

The new interest in tweed had gone mainstream by 2010, with Matt Smith dressed in a tweed jacket as the eleventh Doctor Who. Doc Martens and Nike produced shoes made in tweed, and bespoke tweed garments from Savile Row tailors such as Huntsman or Norton & Sons became increasingly popular.

The Tweed Run, first organized in London in 2009 before spreading to cities around the world, references Victorian cyclists, with tweed jackets and plus fours. It described itself as 'a metropolitan bicycle ride with a bit of style. We take to the streets in our well-pressed best, and cycle through the city's iconic landmarks. Along the way, we stop for a tea break and a picnic stop, and we usually end with a bit of a jolly knees-up.'[17] Another movement for the 2010s was Chaps, as championed through *Chap* magazine, in which the lifestyle of a 1940s' English gentleman was celebrated with vintage tweed, boating blazers, tweed caps and Oxford brogues.[18]

0720

TARTAN, TWEED + ROYALTY

The Queen at the Ghillies Ball, Balmoral in 1971, wearing a Norman Hartnell gown with Stewart tartan sash.

As the fashion leaders of their day, it was the aristocracy of the eighteenth and nineteenth centuries who helped to make tartan and tweed highly fashionable fabrics. Queen Victoria and her love for Balmoral encouraged a huge trend and consumption for tartan. It became the fabric worn by royals when in Scotland, turning visiting European princes into Highland chieftains, and Scotland into a kingdom of tartan romance. Similarly, hardy tweed was worn by landed gentry as they scrambled through the Scottish heath, following a surge in interest in Highland country estates in the nineteenth century.

While it's often imagined that Scottish kings stood proudly in a uniform of tartan, it wasn't until the eighteenth century that tartan became a political symbol. There is little record before then of it being commonly worn or having meaning assigned to it. Before the Jacobite risings, tartan may have been chosen by noblemen and Stewart kings for its style and vivid colours, but such people were more likely to wear the costume of the lowlands, similar to European styles, than the clothes of the Highlands, which had a feudal system practically independent of Crown control.

THE FASHIONS OF THE STEWART COURT

The Royal House of Stewart, or Stuart in the French spelling, is said to have originated from Brittany, while including a mix of Medici blood. Throughout their reigns the Stewarts helped develop Scotland from the feudal Middle Ages to a period of wealth and innovation.

During his reign (1488–1513), James IV encouraged the arts, sciences and splendid building works such as the great halls at Stirling and Edinburgh castles with their huge tapestries. By the time of his death, Europe's Renaissance had brought an interest in fashion to Scotland, and vivid colours and luxury fabrics, a sign of wealth and taste, were greatly influenced by France and Italy.[1] Tartans that were scarlet in colour were the most expensive, and wearing a bright tartan allowed the king to stand out.[2] Contemporary portraits offer the most vivid clues as to what was worn by the ruling kings and noblemen. They tended to be depicted in fashionable European styles, wearing such items as doublets and gilt-embroidered jackets. However, there is an earlier treasurer's record of James III, in 1471, purchasing 'blue Tartane to lyne his gowne of cloth of gold' and 'doble Tartane to lyne ridin collars to her lade the Quene.'[3]

clockwise from top left A royal shooting party at Glamis Castle, Forfarshire, 1921, with the Duke of York and Lady Elizabeth Bows-Lyons in the centre (the future King George VI and Queen Elizabeth); King George V with his three sons, Henry, Edward and George, at Balmoral Castle in 1906; the royals at Balmoral in the 1920s – George Duke of Kent, Queen Mary and the Duke and Duchess of York.

left William Mosman's portrait from 1750 depicts Bonnie Prince Charlie with a boyish face and wearing a tartan jacket, the order of Garter and the Jacobite blue bonnet with white cockade.

above A portrait of Mary Queen of Scots dated around 1565, in an expensive and fashionable gown of the European court.

There is also evidence in the Exchequer records of James V, in 1538, ordering a tartan cloth, or 'Heland tartan', to make a pair of hose, and a varied coloured velvet for the king's short Highland coat, which was to be lined with green taffeta ('variant cullorit veluet to be the Kingis grace ane schort heland coit . . . quarter elne of grene tarratyis to lyne the said coit').[4] With its red and green colours, this would have been a bold, bright costume to befit royalty, and it indicates how fashion had become a statement by the sixteenth century.

There is no evidence that James V's daughter Mary Queen of Scots wore tartan, particularly as she was a French Catholic woman who brought her French wardrobe with her when she arrived in Edinburgh in 1561. Her fine costumes of velvet and silks, embellished with precious stones, pearls and embroidery, would have been awe-inspiring for her subjects.[5] Portraits painted after Mary's death rehabilitated her image as a Catholic martyr, with rosary and crucifixes around her neck, and in black clothes to represent her as a three-times widow. However, there is a description of Mary wearing the clothing of Scotland. The Sieur de Brantome, who knew Mary in the French court, mythologized her great virtue and beauty in his writings, but he also referred to her 'marvelous' image when 'dressed like a savage (as I have seen her) in the barbaric fashion of her country, she still shone forth like a goddess.'[6]

After Mary Queen of Scots was beheaded in 1587, her son, James VI, united the thrones of Scotland and England when becoming James I of England. Following the revolution of 1688, Catholic James VII/II was deposed by Protestant William and Mary, and James Francis Edward Stuart, son of James VII, was exiled, becoming known as the Old Pretender or 'the king over the water'. Supporters would drink to the king's health by passing their glass of whisky over the water jug. James Stuart died in 1766 in Rome, without having met his dream of restoring the Stewarts to the British throne.

Charles Edward, born in 1720, was the son of James Stuart and Clementina Sobieski, a Polish princess. Known as Bonnie Prince Charlie, or the Young Pretender, in 1745 he returned from exile in France to claim his rightful place on the Scottish throne. Early portraits and descriptions conveyed Charles Edward as a young man with a taste for luxurious French fashion, although reports indicated he arrived in Scotland dressed in sombre dark clothing. But with his skills in propaganda, Charles Edward made a dramatic arrival in Edinburgh dressed in a tartan short coat, a blue bonnet and the star of the order of St Andrew on his chest. 'For a few weeks Holyrood House became again what it has so seldom been: a royal palace and a brilliant court', wrote historian Allan Massie. Charles Edward dined in public, rode his horse in front of crowds of spectators, and at Holyrood Abbey he held court for the fashionable ladies of Edinburgh, who may have worn tartan gowns in support.[7]

from top to bottom Swatches of the Royal Stewart, the Stewart Dress and the Stewart Hunting tartans, all official tartans of the royal family.

Following his defeat at Culloden in 1746, when Hanoverian Prince William, Duke of Cumberland, known as 'Cumberland the Butcher', swiftly defeated the Jacobite rising, Scots were banned from wearing Highland dress, ultimately resulting in tartan becoming a political signifier. When something is banned it often becomes even more popular because it is seen to be rebellious, and this was certainly true of tartan. However, by 1789, George III and his descendants were wrapping themselves in tartan as a style statement.[8]

GEORGE IV'S VISIT TO SCOTLAND

It was George IV's triumphant royal visit to Edinburgh in 1822, stage managed by Sir Walter Scott, that inspired a national fascination with tartan. Scott helped to rebrand the king as a British symbol of unity between Scotland and England, by encouraging thousands of Highlanders to welcome the king to Edinburgh in full regalia.[9]

George IV, who was the first Hanoverian to visit Scotland since Culloden, was dressed in full Highland regalia in the Royal Stewart tartan. However, the kilt was too short on the portly king, and his pink tights and belly peeking out from under added comedy to his appearance. The fourth Duke of Atholl, John Murray, described the royal visit as 'one and twenty daft days' and the image of the fat king in Highland dress was depicted in satirical cartoons. However, a painting by Sir David Wilkie unveiled in 1830 to commemorate the visit showed George IV in a more favourable light, wearing the full dress of a clan chieftain, and with muscular legs and arms that added to the image of a mighty presence.

After such a warm welcome, George IV adopted the Royal Stewart as his own personal tartan and as the royal tartan of Great Britain. Different variants of the tartan were created using different colours for Dress, Old and Hunting versions. Dress Stewart tartan, with its white background and extra red line, was Queen Victoria's favourite for evening wear at Balmoral.[10]

VICTORIA AND ALBERT

From their first visit in 1842, Victoria and Albert fell in love with Scotland and they treated it as a 'tartan kingdom of fantasy', according to A.N. Wilson, biographer of Queen Victoria. After arriving at Taymouth Castle they were greeted by a display of pipers, guns and a regiment dressed in Campbell tartan. 'It seemed as if a chieftain in olden feudal times was receiving his sovereign. It was princely and romantic,' Victoria wrote.[11]

When Lord Aberdeen offered to lease the royal couple a small castle in Deeside in 1848, they made the exhausting, sickness-inducing, nine-hour trip to Aberdeen on the royal yacht, and then travelled by horse and cart to reach Balmoral.[12] They both felt completely at home within the hills and forests, the mist and clean air, and the informality compared with life in London.

They bought the castle outright in 1852, and in 1853 the first stone was laid for a bigger castle, designed by Albert. In it, his Bavarian influence is evident with the fairy-tale spires. Balmoral Castle burst with tartan for both costume and interior decoration, and a special Balmoral tartan was designed by Prince Albert for the new castle, with grey, black and red shades to represent the granite landscape of Deeside. It was used for upholstery, curtains and carpets, along with swathes of red Royal Stewart and green Hunting Stewart tartan, creating a nineteenth-century version of the now typical luxury Highland hotel with its tartan furnishings and stags' heads.[13] With the household staff given uniforms of Balmoral tartan and the ghillies of a Balmoral tweed, the castle and its romantic Highland location took on a Disneyland-esque corporate identity.

Albert would typically wear a kilt while hunting and for formal occasions, while Victoria wore a long silk tartan scarf almost every evening at Balmoral, her luxury version of the arisaid.

For a torchlight ball at Corriemulzie in September 1852, Victoria described their outfits: 'I wore a white bonnet, a grey watered silk and (according to Highland fashion) my plaid scarf over my shoulder; and Albert his Highland dress which he wears every evening . . . it was really a most beautiful and unusual sight. All the company were assembled there. A space about one hundred feet in length and sixty feet in width was boarded, and entirely surrounded by Highlanders bearing torches . . . all the Highland gentlemen and any who were at all Scotch, were in kilts, the ladies in evening dresses.'[14]

Despite having a limited interest in clothes, Victoria helped make tartan the height of fashion for wealthy women, even down to their undergarments, as revealed by a lady-in-waiting to Queen Victoria, the Honourable Eleanor Stanley. She wrote in 1859 of an embarrassing incident for the Duchess of Manchester who caught a hoop of her cage when trying to climb over a stile, and 'went regularly head over heels lighting on her feet with her cage and whole petticoats remaining above her head . . . the other ladies hardly knew whether to be thankful or not that a part of her underclothing consisted in a pair of scarlet tartan knickerbockers'.[15]

The Victoria influence inspired wide fashion trends for tartan as underskirts or worn overdress in silk and wools, and it was noted in the 1937 book *English Women's Clothing in the Nineteenth Century* that in 1869

left top to bottom Princess Helena and Princess Louise, Queen Victoria's daughters, in 1856, wearing matching tartan dresses; photograph from 1856 by Roger Fenton of a ghillie on the Balmoral estate, wearing the uniform Balmoral tartan kilt and tweed jacket.

right Princess Margaret and Princess Elizabeth in matching kilts in the gardens of Windsor Castle in 1936.

'tartan is the fashion and must be worn' and, in 1871, tartan was widely worn in tribute to the marriage of Princess Louise, fourth daughter of the queen.[16]

In 1878 Victoria purchased the Forest of Ballochbuie, where, according to myth, clan Farquharson bought the land from clan MacGregor in exchange for tartan plaid. In tribute to this story Victoria planted a stone with the words: 'The bonniest plaid in Scotland.'[17]

Victoria and Albert's son, Edward VII (known as Bertie), was dressed in little Scotch suits as a child, and this outfit of kilt and dress jacket became very popular for children after he wore it at the Great Exhibition opening in 1851 and then at the wedding of Victoria, the Princess Royal in 1858. Prince Albert was often frustrated that Bertie was a playboy prince with little interest in politics, history and architecture, complaining that Bertie 'takes no interest in anything but clothes and again clothes.'[18]

THE FASHIONABLE PRINCE OF WALES

Bertie's name would be associated with a checked fabric known as the glen check, or the Prince of Wales. With his fashion-conscious flair, Bertie wore checked tweed suits for shooting, made from the cloth he had been given on a visit to the Outer Hebrides. His son George V and grandson Edward, Prince of Wales, later the Duke of Windsor (after his abdication in 1936), would also wear tweed as an outdoor sports cloth, setting a tradition for those with the title of Prince of Wales to be celebrated for their sense of style. This was noted in the *New York Times* in 1929, at the height of fascination for Edward, Prince of Wales. 'In nearly all reigns the Prince of Wales has been famous as a creator of men's fashions. It was the greatest joy of George IV, who spent most of his life as Prince of Wales, to call in his tailors to design new coats and pantaloons, and

below left The Duke of Windsor photographed for *Vogue* in 1964 at his home in Paris, in one of his 'loud' checked suits.

below The Duke of Windsor with Wallis Simpson in the late 1930s, wearing his daring combination of tweed suit and bold tie in a Windsor knot.

when he died he left literarily hundreds of waistcoats which he had never worn.'[19]

At that time Edward, Prince of Wales was the most fashionable man on the planet. He was the most popular member of the royal family and was known for his charm and boyish looks. He would be greeted with cheerful enthusiasm wherever in the world he visited. As next in line to the throne the prince knew he could push the boundaries and break the rules of dress, just as he rebelled against authority – by dropping out of Oxford University because he couldn't stand the rules and, ultimately, by abdicating in order to marry the woman he loved – Wallis Simpson.[20]

Reflective of the new era after the First World War, Edward was the first heir to the British throne whose image could be spread by photography, movies and media, and his rebellious style was partly owed to the jazz age, a time of experimentation and carefree behaviour. He argued with his parents over modern trends – jazz, cocktails, trouser turn-ups and talking on the telephone.[21] He liked anything that was new and modern, and, as Wallis Simpson discovered, had a particular penchant for Americans.

He chose to take fashion risks such as wearing a Glengarry bonnet in an unconventional way, inventing the 'Windsor knot' and combining a morning suit with a blue shirt and vivid blue tie, which had never been done before. He abolished frock coats from court and, because he didn't like the military wardrobes and constant changes he was expected to wear on state visits, he chose to wear linen, jodhpurs and safari suits when touring India or Australia. Yet he was also partial to tradition. For evening entertaining at his country home, Fort Belvedere, the prince dressed in a kilt to host cocktails before dinner. He had rows of kilts in his wardrobe in his favourite tartans of Royal and Hunting Stewart, Balmoral and Lord of the Isles. Noted fashion columnist and editor Diana Vreeland once commented that the prince 'had style in every buckle on his kilt, every check of his country suits.'[22]

Edward's style was very much the dandy of the 1920s, with a sportswear look that would be the instigator of the Ivy League look on American college campuses – Harris Tweed jackets, patched shooting suits, a Fair Isle vest, plus fours and Argyll socks for golf. The left pocket of his checked golfing trousers, designed by H. Harris of New York, was always cut slightly wider to accommodate a cigarette case.[23]

The prince's wardrobe, while large, was also frugal. He demonstrated how sturdy a tweed jacket could be by wearing one of his father's Rothesay hunting suits dating from 1897. In 1960 the now Duke of Windsor wrote of his grandfather, Bertie's, generation: 'They and my father wore even their tweeds, as they did their other clothes, not with a view to relaxation but as a costume dictated by custom for a particular purpose.'[24] The duke instead chose to wear tartan and tweed the

'They and my father wore even their tweeds, as they did their other clothes, not with a view to relaxation but as a costume dictated by custom for a particular purpose.' The Duke of Windsor

American way, such as the Palm Beach look of tartan trousers or beach shorts with checked shirts.

Although his wife Wallis Simpson was not necessarily a fan of his 'very loud checked tweeds', as she referred to them in her autobiography,[25] this eccentric sense of style stayed with Edward throughout his life. Even in exile after his abdication he kept his links to the Crown by wearing aspects of formal Highland dress, and he was photographed by Lord Lichfield in the 1960s while wearing a checked shirt, tartan trousers, paisley cravat and argyle socks.

Another trendsetting royal in the 1930s was Princess Marina. She helped boost British textiles struggling under the depression, by wearing Scottish tweeds and lace. A Duchess of Kent tartan was designed in 1934 especially for her, and she was one of the first of the modern royals whose style was noted in magazines.[26]

THE WINDSORS

Following the abdication in 1936, the new king, George VI, was keen to go back to the stability of the Victorian era, and so encouraged the image of his queen and two daughters to use British fabrics and a Victorian aesthetic. 'After the constitutional crisis, and his suddenly becoming king, which was unexpected, there was a period where, if we look back with hindsight, we can see that there was a certain amount of image making going on and it was around this time that Queen Elizabeth, the Queen's mother, began to use Norman Hartnell as a designer', said fashion historian Caroline de Guitaut.[27]

With her fondness for soft pastels, Queen Elizabeth (the Queen Mother) could never match Wallis Simpson, with her angular lines and Parisian-chic fashions, in the style stakes. For times spent in Balmoral Elizabeth wore her safe, practical tweed jackets and tartan skirts which she called 'old friends' – 'you never get rid of old friends'.[28]

The two princesses, Elizabeth and Margaret, became the royal style icons in the following decades. They were photographed in tweed jackets and jodhpurs picking daffodils in Windsor Park, in April 1940, and at Balmoral in the obligatory tartan pleated skirt. Once she had acceded to the throne in 1952, the now Elizabeth II understood how her wardrobe must speak for diplomacy, with colours that allowed her to stand out in a crowd, skirts long enough to cover her knees when sitting down, and on state visits outfits that combined touches that paid tribute to the country she was visiting.[29] Tartan acts as a diplomatic message when in Scotland, while also referencing the queen's Scottish heritage as her mother had been born at Glamis Castle.[30]

There is an example in the Royal Collection of a Norman Hartnell evening dress of embroidered duchesse satin with a sash of Royal Stewart tartan, worn by the queen at the Ghillies Ball at Balmoral Castle in 1971. The Ghillies Ball was originally introduced by Victoria in the 1850s, and it's where neighbours and estate workers are invited for a celebration at the castle.

above Queen Elizabeth II, Prince Philip, Princess Anne and Prince Charles at Balmoral in August 1952. The Queen wears her favoured Balmoral style of pleated tartan skirt and tweed jacket.

above right Queen Elizabeth II watching the horses in Gloucestershire in April 1968.

right The Prince of Wales was considered the inheritor of his uncle the Duke of Windsor's impeccable style when it came to relaxed menswear.

far right Charles and Diana pose for photographers during their honeymoon at Balmoral. Diana updated the traditions of country estate tweed with a Bill Pashley hunting suit.

By tradition, the ladies wear long gowns and a sash of Royal Stewart, and the men are in Highland dress.

Having spent her summer holiday at Balmoral since the year she was born, in 1926, Queen Elizabeth II has kept the routine the same, despite being as 'off duty' as she can be. She enjoyed bagpipes as a morning wake-up call, picnics at the same gamekeepers huts, steaks grilled by Philip, scones and sausage rolls, and fishing on the river Dee. Off-duty dressing in Balmoral for the queen since the 1950s has been a skirt in her own private Balmoral tartan, a tweed or Barbour jacket and wellies.[31]

When Lady Diana Spencer was first invited to Balmoral in 1980, a year before her marriage to Prince Charles, she found the traditions and routines intimidating. Being able to take part in country pursuits, and to be appropriately dressed in the right tweeds, were vitally important, but fortuitously Diana could keep up with the outdoor way of life. As Tina Brown wrote in her biography of Diana: 'It was a big plus to Diana's cause that she appeared so happy tramping over sodden moors . . . without fresh-air credentials, Diana would have never got past round one with any of them.'[32]

Diana had a tendency to go for New Romantic ruffles, pie-crust collars and feathered hats, but for visits to Scotland appropriate outfits in tartan and tweed were chosen. On their honeymoon at Balmoral in 1981, and with the world's press watching, Diana and Prince Charles posed for photographs with the prince in a kilt (in the Rothesay tartan), sporran and V-neck jumper and Diana wearing a sophisticated tweed hunting suit designed by Bill Pashley, marking her acceptance within the family.

Going to the Braemar Games was a highlight of the Balmoral calendar. As part of the traditional royal look in Scotland, Diana in 1981 wore a button-down tartan dress with frilled collar, designed by Sloane Ranger favourite Caroline Charles, with a Glengarry bonnet designed by John Boyd. Another gown belonging to Diana that showcased tartan was a Catherine Walker dress with a black velvet bodice and long green, black and red silk tartan skirt, for a night of dancing at Balmoral.[33]

Wearing tartan and tweeds has continued to be an enduring tradition, with every member of the royal family encouraged to wear tartan on visits to Scotland. The tartans are created by royal warrant holders Kinloch Anderson. Prince Charles wears a kilt in Lord of the Isles or Rothesay tartan in reference to his titles, while the Duke of Edinburgh had previously worn the Cameron tartan as Colonel in Chief to the Queen's Own Cameron Highlanders.[34]

Prince Charles' daughter-in-law Catherine (Kate) Middleton has now stepped into her role as royal style icon. She chooses tweed and tartan coats for their warmth and conservative practicality on walkabouts, or touches of Strathearn tartan to represent her title in Scotland as the wife of Prince William, who is the Earl of Strathearn.

following pages Princess Diana wearing a Caroline Charles tartan dress at the Braemar Games in 1981, with Charles in a kilt of Rothesay tartan; the Windsors in their country outfits at the Badminton Horse Trials in Gloucestershire.

A BUYER'S GUIDE TO TARTAN

Since tartan is a fabric with international appeal, men and women across the globe are keen to secure a piece of their own, yet the prospect of buying tartan can seem like a minefield with such a great number of traditional and fashion-led designs on offer. No longer is the kilt associated with wild marshes but instead with celebration, occasion and patriotism, often seen at weddings, dinners and graduations and worn proudly by pipe bands and Highland dancers. Largely aligned with specific clans, tartan patterns themselves are often presented as accurate reflections of the original designs worn by the clans throughout history. The direct link between individual tartan designs and their corresponding clan names can be ambiguous and it's unlikely that the designs like those we see today were worn by Scots before the early nineteenth century. Despite the historical disparity, buying tartan is made easier if you have a firm grasp on the language used to describe this fabric and an understanding of the most popular patterns, or setts.

TYPES OF TARTAN

From the outset we can dispel the myth that you need to be Scottish to wear tartan and, whilst it's customary to wear your own clan tartan, these rules have been greatly relaxed and there are universal tartans that can be worn by anyone. Traditionally a buyer would begin with their last name, or consider district tartans if their surname was not linked to a specific clan. The Scottish Register of Tartans is the official tartan database and records all setts currently available. There you will note tartans are denoted by clan name, district, corporation, a special event, a fashion brand, the military and royalty.

Tartan exists in hundreds of colours and setts, but like any fabric there are key combinations that have particular cultural or historical significance or have proved to be popular commercially. When a fabric enjoys worldwide popularity it will typically be reinvented to suit the needs and tastes of societies and occasions across the globe. Modern colour combinations are achieved by using chemical dyes (natural dyes were used until the mid-nineteenth century). According to tartan historian Peter Macdonald: 'After the mid-nineteenth century chemical dyes offered a cheap, quicker and easier way of obtaining standard colours albeit often to the detriment of the original patterns where the design subtleties often became obscured.'[1]

Most tartans have a Modern and an Ancient version, with the latter typically referring to the same tartan made in lighter colours to replicate the fabric ageing over time. For first-time buyers there's a common misconception that Ancient tartans are older than

Modern ones, but these names often refer to the colours rather than the age of the tartan. It is the sett that identifies a tartan and there can be several variations of one design depending on the colours used. Hunting tartans are traditionally made up of greens, blues and browns and are only connected to certain clans. Armstrong or Campbell, for example, do not have Hunting tartans because their standard clan tartan is already in these colours. The term 'hunting' therefore refers to the tartan's colours rather than the age of the fabric or the pursuits the wearer might undertake whilst wearing it. For formal occasions Dress tartans are widely worn but there is no steadfast rule that other derivations of tartan such as Hunting or Modern cannot be worn. Again, the term 'dress' refers only to the colours used within the fabric. In this case white is traditionally a primary colour with standard tartans being altered to include extra white within their designs.

The wearer should not be afraid to choose a tartan that isn't connected to their family name. The rules of Highland dress are governed only by personal taste so choosing the design that catches your attention is advisable rather than searching for an intangible genetic connection. According to Matthew Newsome: 'fashion tartan is a tartan that is produced and worn without any authorization from a governing agent. By that I mean the chief in regard to clan tartans, or a CEO for a corporate tartan, or a local government for a district tartan. Tartans with the express approval of such an authority are "official" in the sense that they are authorized by the body they are meant to represent. If a tartan has no approval, it is termed a fashion tartan'.[2]

CHOOSING A TARTAN

With thousands of tartans to choose from, finding a favourite pattern can take time so industry experts recommend selecting a tartan that has personal significance – an important location, a selection of colours or links to a family name. Every tartan has a complex and often conflicting history, so it is not uncommon to confuse similar tartan designs. For example, the Black Watch and Campbell tartan appear to be one and the same, although the Campbell tartan has many deviations linked to various branches of the clan including Campbell of Cawdor, Campbell of Breadalbane and Campbell of Glenlyon, each possessing its own characteristics. Aid your search with this brief overview of popular tartans and find more on pages 198–205.

BALMORAL

The Balmoral tartan was created to complement the Royal Stewart and Hunting Stewart tartans used to decorate the interior of Queen Victoria and Prince Albert's home on the Balmoral estate. Designed by Prince Albert himself in 1853, the sett has a grey background (said to represent the granite found in Royal Deeside) and features red and black checks with black and white thread twisted together through the background to achieve a textured appearance. The royal couple fell in love with their residence at Balmoral and spent a substantial amount of time there, meanwhile promoting the Highland activities in their midst. Traditionally the Balmoral tartan can only be worn by those of royal lineage and Queen Elizabeth II is often photographed in Balmoral tartan skirts. One notable exception to the rule is the Queen's personal piper who often wears Balmoral tartan for ceremonial occasions.

GORDON

Often associated with Highland regiments, the Gordon tartan is derived from the Black Watch tartan but includes a yellow stripe for differentiation and was designed by local tartan manufacturer William Forsyth. One of the most prominent clans in north-east Scotland in the sixteenth and seventeenth centuries, the Gordons were originally named Adam and were wealthy landowners. As an active supporter of King Robert I (Robert the Bruce), Sir Adam of Gordon negotiated with the Pope to reverse Bruce's excommunication. As a reward for their loyalty Robert the Bruce gave the Gordons land in Strathbogie, Aberdeenshire. Their castle became known as Huntly and Clan Gordon subsequently became one of the most powerful families in the north-east of Scotland. During the Reformation, the Gordons fought for Mary Queen of Scots, resulting in George Gordon, fourth Earl of Huntly, dying in battle and his son being beheaded. At the Jacobite Risings of 1715 and 1745 there were Gordons on both sides - the second Duke of Gordon followed the Jacobites in 1715 but by 1745 the third duke supported the Hanoverians. In 1794 the fourth Duke of Gordon established the 92nd Gordon Highlanders who became famous for their charge at the Battle of Waterloo.

BRUCE OF KINNAIRD

Worn by a branch of the Bruce clan, this tartan was taken from an eighteenth-century coat owned by the Bruces of Kinnaird. Authorized for wear around 1953 by Lord Bruce of Kinnaird, this sett is influenced by both the Old Bruce tartan and the Prince Charles

Edward Stuart tartan. James Bruce of Kinnaird was a respected explorer who reportedly discovered the source of the Blue Nile and was nicknamed 'The Abyssinian'. More recently this colourful tartan has been favoured by fashion designers who are attracted by its vibrant shades of khaki green, orange, pink, white, yellow and black. It was most famously used by Vivienne Westwood for an Ancient Bruce of Kinnaird tartan dancing jacket that appeared on Westwood's first British *Vogue* cover in November 1989. Later in 1993, Westwood's Anglomania autumn/winter collection featured several Bruce of Kinnaird tartan pieces including an eye-catching, double-breasted coat, waistcoat and trousers.

MACKENZIE

The Mackenzie's were at the height of their power in the sixteenth century but later struggled to recover after supporting the Jacobite rebellion in 1715. By the second Jacobite rising in 1745, Clan Mackenzie was divided with Kenneth Mackenzie (Lord Fortrose) aligned with the British government and George Mackenzie (third Earl of Cromartie) with the Jacobites. Known for its military connections, the Mackenzie tartan was worn by the 72nd Seaforth Highlanders who fought in India, the Crimea and Afghanistan. Derived from the Black Watch tartan, the Mackenzie sett typically features black, white and red lines. It has been suggested that an alternative Mackenzie tartan existed before 1700 that was predominantly red but was lost in the years after the Battle of Culloden and replaced by the popular military version that we know today. It is associated with one of Scotland's most iconic castles, as the Mackenzies once held Eilean Donan Castle as a long-term seat. The modern seat of Clan Mackenzie – Castle Leod – was thought to be the inspiration behind 'Castle Leoch' in the popular *Outlander* television series.

FRASER

The Fraser tartan was listed in the Sobieskis' *Vestiarium Scoticum* and according to the Scottish Register of Tartans is in fact 'an early Grant tartan which he [D.W. Stewart] traced to a portrait of Robert Grant of Lurg (1678–1771) hanging at the Troup House before it was closed around 1894.'[3] The clan is divided into two main branches – The Frasers of Lovat (Inverness-shire) and The Frasers of Philorth (Aberdeenshire). The Frasers of Lovat tartan was reportedly woven by Wilson's of Bannockburn around 1820 and is slightly different from the original Fraser tartan. The Fraser Hunting tartan is thought to have relatively obscure origins, having been woven by the Sobieski Stuarts, who were reportedly commissioned by Lord

Lovat. Rather than being taken directly from their *Vestiarium Scoticum*, this particular tartan was specifically altered in shades of brown at the request of their benefactor for military use.

BUYING A KILT

The nuances of kilt wearing are more intricate than one might expect. There are many schools of thought when it comes to fabric length and width but all are agreed that when purchasing your first kilt it's best to choose a reputable kilt-maker. In days of old, before the industrial revolution, Scots gave little thought to tartan names and the cultural references of individual patterns. Today most kilt buyers select a tartan that has some personal significance, typically attributed to family heritage. Nevertheless the process can easily become confusing when Dress, Hunting and Modern versions of the preferred tartan are on offer.

A standard-quality kilt is heavy, durable and traditionally 7.3 metres/8 yards in length, while 'casual kilts' and 'hillwalking kilts' of 3.65 metres/4 yards are now available. Traditional kilt wearers might disapprove of these modern reinterpretations, yet it is widely acknowledged that the kilts of the eighteenth and nineteenth centuries were made of little more than 3.65 metres/4 yards. Tartan fabric tends to come in three weights and categories: light (312 grams/11 ounces); medium (368 grams/13 ounces); and heavy (454–482 grams/16–17 ounces). Traditionalists often choose a 454-gram/16-ounce heavyweight cloth for a kilt as the pleats are said to sit and swing better, but lightweight fabric is also acceptable. Scrimping on quality is ill advised when it comes to kilts so invest in the best you can afford. Lower-priced kilts are unlikely to stand the test of time and will cost more in the long term when they need to be replaced or altered because they've been poorly constructed. Before shopping with unrecognized suppliers consider the level of workmanship involved in creating a high-quality kilt. Kilts are finely crafted products - from chalking the fabric, to hand-stitching pleats, attaching buckles and belt loops and sewing inner linings - every stage is carefully considered and worth investing in.

The most important factor to get right is the kilt's length. At its longest the traditional kilt should reach to the top of the kneecap. The Victorians wore their kilts on the middle of the kneecap but this is considered old-fashioned. You will note that the bottom of the kilt is the selvedge of the fabric meaning there is no hem to alter the length of the kilt after the fabric is cut. Bearing that in mind, the most crucial kilt measurement is from the hip bone to the top of the knee cap which should determine the kilt's length. Waist and seat measurements can be tricky, depending on the fit of kilt required, but typically the waist measurement is taken to the tightest parameter as the belt buckle allows for adjustments to be made if the kilt's waistline feels too tight. The seat measurement is taken over a shirt and the largest part of the seat. Two straps hold the kilt in place on the outside and a third strap is often included on the inside to hold the various layers together. According to the Scottish Tartans Authority: 'Highland dress isn't preserved in aspic, it's a living, evolving fashion and adding one's own distinctive touches to it prevents us all becoming homogenized . . . as long as the touches don't belittle the dress that you're wearing and cause offence to others who hold their heritage dear.'

DRESSING THE KILT

Kilt accessories

Traditionally hose (socks) should be worn above the calf but 5–7 centimentres/ 2–3 inches below the lower knee. Hose are typically worn in muted colours of grey, navy, dark green and black but are also available in white. Underneath the fold of the hose, garter flashes are worn with the elastic tucked beneath the fold and the coloured fabric seen on the outside of the leg. On the feet, evening brogues or ghillie brogues are worn with long laces that tie around the ankles. Originally, the addition of laces meant that the wearer wouldn't lose his shoes on uneven muddy ground, and still provide security when twisted four times around the ankle and tied at the front. Traditionalists are typically highly regimented when it comes to kilt accessories and 'The purists insist on polished black shoes with the kilt but this is probably a hangover from service regulations. There is nothing dreadfully wrong with brown shoes or even suede.'[4] Lastly the kilt pin is less functional than one might expect, existing for ornamentation alone and not meant to keep kilt flaps closed. Attached only to the front apron, the kilt pin should not snag the fabric or cause the corresponding side to dip lower than the rest of the kilt.

The Sporran and Sgian dubh

Unless you're at a sporting event it's rare to see the kilt worn without a sporran. Once a large, impractical accessory, modern sporrans are highly refined and widely available in leather or fur. Sporrans are typically classified in three categories – day, semi-dress and dress – although the lines of distinction are rather blurred and etiquette surrounding the different types of sporran is not so closely followed by modern gentlemen. The sporran should be large enough to hold a money clip for bills, space for a credit card and a coin purse and room for house or car keys. The sporran strap should be put through the loops at the back of the kilt, and the chains brought forward to attach them to the rings at the rear of the sporran. The hang of the sporran is adjusted by means of the rear strap and buckle to ensure that it's worn high and not midway down the front apron. To conform with traditional etiquette: 'The top of a small sporran should not be lower than about a hand's breadth below your navel.'[5] The sgian dubh (Gaelic for 'black knife') was once used by Highlanders as a means of self-defence and is the finishing touch to the kilt outfit (albeit an optional rather than mandatory addition). Purely ornamental, the modern sgian dubh has a stainless-steel blade and is tucked into the right sock with the handle within easy reach.

CARING FOR YOUR KILT

Quality kilts are not cheap so if investing hard-earned cash in a kilt it's worth looking after it. Store the kilt on a clamp hanger rather than hanging it by its internal loops, which will cause the kilt to sag and loose its shape over time. If the kilt is damp make sure it dries out completely before covering it with a garment bag and storing in a well-ventilated room. Check for any stains that might tarnish the fabric. Many kilt cleaners use a simple clean cloth and warm water to remove any stains but do test any cleaning products on the inside of the kilt to make sure a bigger mark does not appear. Lastly, don't forget to remove the kilt pin before storing the kilt because they can rust and ruin the fabric.

clockwise from left A Givenchy coat in MacQueen tartan; Alexander McQueen with Sarah Jessica Parker at the Anglomania Met Costume Institute Benefit Gala in 2006; R.R McIan's depiction of the MacDonald of Keppoch costume.

MACQUEEN

THE REBEL TARTAN

With its vivid red, black and yellow sett, MacQueen tartan is one of the most striking and with its links to the bold red tartans in Jacobite portraiture, it has taken on a rebellious reputation.

Alexander McQueen often used a slight adaptation of the MacQueen tartan to signify Scottish rebellion against oppression following the Jacobite uprisings. With his Highland Rape collection in 1995, McQueen subverted the clanship symbol of tartan through violent imagery, with slashed and bloodied fabric to present the 'rape' of Scotland by greedy landowners in the eighteenth and nineteenth centuries. McQueen's follow-up to this was his Widows of Culloden collection in 2006, with anglicized versions of Scottish dress designed to show how the failed Jacobite rebellion and the Battle of Culloden destroyed the Highland way of life.

McQueen also saw the tartan as a link to his own history, traced to the Isle of Skye, where the Clan MacQueen defended their land and family. The MacQueen clan are of Viking origin, when Norsemen settled on the Hebrides in the ninth and tenth centuries. With a heritage born from the powerful Gaelic Clan Donald, they formed a confederation with the MacDonald and MacKintosh clans called Clan Chattan. It is said that the MacQueens were guards at the marriage between the daughter of the chief of Clan Ranald and the chief of Clan MacKintosh.

Because of these ties, when the tartan was first recorded in the MacKintosh *Vestiarium Scoticum* in 1842, it was very similar to that of the MacDonald and MacKintosh clans and was described as 'fowr stryppis red vpon ane blak fylde, and throuchout ye mydward of ye blak sett, ane zello spraing'.

clockwise from top left A derivation of the Black Watch kilt; Glasgow tram conductors during the First World War wearing uniforms with Black Watch skirts; Black Watch street style; The McQ Alexander McQueen show at London Fashion Week autumn/winter 2012/2013.

BLACK WATCH

THE MILITARY TARTAN

Also known as the Government tartan, the Hanoverian tartan and the Universal tartan, the blue, green and black checks of the Black Watch have made an impressive sight over the centuries when worn in battle. The Highland regiments, with their kilts and Glengarry bonnets, were sent on overseas campaigns to defend the British colonies in North America and India, and to fight in the Battle of Waterloo, the Crimean War and the First and Second World Wars.

The Black Watch can be traced back to 1725 when the government set up six independent companies to patrol areas of the Highlands to prevent cattle rustling, often used for blackmail. They were instructed to wear similar green, blue and black tartans to keep a sense of uniformity, and it became known as the Government tartan by 1739.[1] Because three of the six original regiments were under Clan Campbell, the Black Watch tartan would later be adapted as the clan tartan of the Campbells and officially adopted by the Black Watch Highland Regiment in 1881 until it was disbanded in 2006, and stripped of its identity.

In fashion, the Black Watch's regimental, uniform look makes it a choice for schoolgirl skirts and pinafores, and as a dark and dramatic tartan for kilts. Black Watch featured in the McQ autumn/winter 2012/2013 collection by Sarah Burton, with military-style coats and dresses that reflected the sett's armed forces connection. Kate Middleton wore a modified version of the Black Watch McQ coat on St Andrew's Day when visiting St Andrews University.[2]

left Topman Design show at the London collections, autumn/winter 2015/2016; ***right*** A$AP Rocky in New York, 2013.

MACLEOD
THE DARING TARTAN

The bright yellow and black of the MacLeod tartan is bold, vibrant and commands attention, making it the choice of tartan for fashion designers who wish to make a daring statement. The MacLeod of Lewis yellow and black checks with the red stripe is even known as 'loud MacLeod'. For a more muted version, the MacLeod Hunting tartan has green and blue checks with a red and yellow stripe.

The MacLeod clan are from the Isle of Lewis, coming from the Vikings who arrived in the Outer Hebrides and Skye in the eleventh century, and were descended from Leod. By 1829, during the fashion for recording clan tartans, MacLeod of Dunvegan claimed this tartan as the MacLeod clan tartan, with its 'three black stryps upon ain yellow fylde.'[1]

MacLeod is the tartan that can make an impact: for example, the narrow, Topman, Noddy Holder-style suits in 2015; grungy MacLeod plaid shirts in Danish designer Asger Juel Larsen's collection in 2014; on Victoria's Secret bras in 2013; in Jean Paul Gaultier punk plaid dresses and trench coats as worn by Rihanna; and in popular Vivienne Westwood corseted dresses.

clockwise from left Punk fashion at the Rebellion Punk Festival, Blackpool, 2010; Donna Karan, autumn/winter 1994/1995 in New York; Dolce & Gabbana, autumn/winter 2008/2009 at Milan Fashion Week.

STEWART

THE PUNK TARTAN

Stewart tartan has rock'n'roll status as a fabric worn by punks, pop and glam rock stars, and is probably the most recognizable tartan in the world. There are in fact more than a hundred Stewart tartans registered in the Tartan Index but the Royal Stewart is the most prolific - its red, green and white stripes are printed on shortbread tins and Scotch bonnets, while the Dress Stewart, with its prominent white overstripes, is commonly used for more formal wear.

Royal Stewart tartan was perhaps the preferred fabric for punks because it was so easily available from charity shops and bargain bins. A kilt could be customized and modified and the safety pin appropriated for use elsewhere. The tartan also acted as a symbol both of rebellion and of the Establishment. The Royal Stewart is the queen's official tartan, while also championed by rebels during the Jacobite uprisings, who fought for the House of Stewart.

Stewart Tartan has been incorporated into fashion lines by Donna Karan in 1994, with playful dresses and hats, by Dolce & Gabbana in 2008 (inspired by Queen Elizabeth II and the Highlands)[1] and by Jean Paul Gaultier, who has played with tartan throughout his career and created punky, Stewart mini-kilts for Madonna's Drowned World tour stage costumes. But it's Vivienne Westwood who brought the punk meaning to the Stewart tartan, and has returned to using it in many collections throughout her career.

A BUYER'S GUIDE TO TWEED

Tweed is one of the most durable of fabrics. With its high-twist fibres creating a tough, impenetrable barrier, tweed's thorn-proof qualities mean that it is ideally suited for tramping through the undergrowth, while the lanolin in wool means that water runs off it and it dries quickly. To enhance the protective quality of tweed, it can be given a coating, or be lined with Gortex. A good-quality jacket made from tweed is also environmentally friendly as it is expected to last for decades, making it the type of clothing that can be passed on down through the generations.

The texture of tweed comes down to the different yarns and techniques that have been used. Pure carded wool is a heavier type of wool, and adds a richness of colour and texture, and when wool is combined with cashmere or merino it creates a sheen to the fabric.

Different regions of Scotland provide different types of tweed, which vary depending on the breed of sheep and the tightness of the weave. One of the main differences between tweeds from the Outer Hebrides and those from the Scottish Borders is that Borders tweed has a flatter look, while Hebrides tweed has a thick, rougher finish to it.

There are also popular tweed manufacturing areas in Italy: for example, in the Biella region, the tweed has a softer, lighter texture because of the area's warmer climate, and it is popular with fashion houses such as Armani. In comparison to Italian tweed, Scottish tweed is often more rugged, partly because it suits the environment, but also because of the thicker wool and the water that is available.

BORDERS TWEED

Borders tweed has a lighter, smoother feel than Hebrides tweed and the tight weave provides a thorn-proof fabric, which makes it ideal for gamekeepers. Such tweed was popular for hunting outfits of plus fours and jackets as it was ideal for crawling about on the ground while deerstalking. It is a tight weave, and the tighter the weave, the more there is a defined pattern.

Borders tweed is traditionally made from the wool of the Cheviot, a white-faced sheep found on the hills of Northumberland and in the Scottish Borders. The yarn is thick and rough, and has a firmness allowing it to be woven tightly, to create a smoother finish for good drapes.

HEBRIDES TWEED

The Isle of Harris is the source of one of the most enduring and popular of tweeds. Originally worked on handlooms, it is coarser and less tightly woven than other tweeds. It could also be

NIKE
NIKE

described as 'hairy' when compared with Borders tweed. Because of its rougher quality, Harris Tweed often has stronger colouring.

The wool of Harris Tweed was traditionally from blackface sheep, which have a strong, bulky, coarse fleece to suit the harsh environment. The Cheviots in the Borders are less exposed to the elements, and so have a softer, thicker, longer fleece.[1]

SHETLAND TWEED

The wool of sheep on Shetland is soft and delicate, making a tight, thin tweed. The Shetland sheep, closely related to the now-extinct Scottish Dunface, are known for being adaptable and able to survive in harsh conditions.

TYPES OF TWEED PATTERNING

The texture of the tweed produces a rugged and authentic look, as well as muting the colours. A tartan pattern can be used in a tweed fabric for this more muted look. Other patterns of tweed that you will commonly find include the following.

Barleycorn tweeds are typically coarse and have a weave that produces the effect of barley kernels when viewed close-up.

Bird's-eye tweed has little points or flecks of contrasting twill, which can provide a colourful, lively texture.

Donegal tweed is a type of tweed produced in County Donegal, Ireland, but it has its own distinctive pattern, where the cloth is formed with different-coloured warp and weft, and is dotted with flecks of colour at irregular intervals for a rough, speckled effect.

Estate tweeds are specially commissioned tweeds which act as a form of branding for a particular estate, creating a uniform for the estate's ghillies and keepers. The book *Scottish Estate Tweeds* (1995) offers a comprehensive list, and it notes that Glenfeshie was one of the earliest estate tweeds to be commissioned, in 1835.[2] When designing their Balmoral tartan, Victoria and Albert also designed Balmoral tweed in the same colourings, for estate workers to wear.

Gamekeeper tweed is stereotypically the fabric worn by academics. As a cloth with a heavier weight, it was the ideal fabric for gamekeepers as it provided extra warmth and protection from the weather.

Glen check, or Prince of Wales check, is common for men's suit jackets. It found popularity in the 1950s for Ivy League style and businessmen (see also page 219).

Gun club check takes its name from either a New York or Baltimore gun club, which took up the Coigach estate tweed in 1874 but adapted it with alternating dark lines and a pale line to create the contrasting checks (see also page 217). These were traditional in the dark brown, gold and green colours of the west coast. Don Draper in *Mad Men* wore a gun check sports jacket for a scene set in 1964.

Herringbone, also known as broken twill weave, is one of the most popular patterns for tweed, particularly in outdoor wear, and it consists of a fine v-shape or zigzag. Its name comes from the way the 'v' pattern looks like fish bones (see also page 215). There are many different variations of herringbone, including wide, fine, tram and window-pane check.

Houndstooth originated in the Scottish Borders and is characterized by its abstract pattern of four-pointed shapes, created by alternating bands of four dark and four light threads in both warp and weft (see also page 221). Black and white is often used for an even greater contrast. Houndstooth can also be referred to as dogtooth and puppytooth – names that differentiate the size of the check.

Overcheck is when a large checked design in contrasting colour is woven over a plain twill or a herringbone design.

HOW TO LOOK AFTER YOUR TWEED

Paul Walker from Walker Slater in Edinburgh advises: 'Keep it in a suit bag as moths are the biggest killer of tweed. Don't put away when wet, and avoid dry cleaning as it doesn't help the oils in wool. Air it out and put out on the washing line to keep it fresh. Do not put your tweed in the washing machine as it will distort the shape of the garment, and the wool is likely to shrink.'[3]

When choosing a tweed, think about what you want to do with it – is it to be worn outside, is it for an event or special occasion? For the Glorious Twelfth, for example, a light summer tweed is traditionally worn. You should also take into account whether you will be wearing the tweed indoors, in which case you don't want it to be too heavy and warm. Some of the styles of jacket include the very traditional Norfolk jacket, or a heavy overcoat such as a guards coat.

Also consider the fit of the jacket, and whether this should be elegant and slim, or a more robust fit. Once you have chosen the fit, you can then consider the colouring and which tones suit you – some people look better in greys and blues, while others are better with yellow tones.

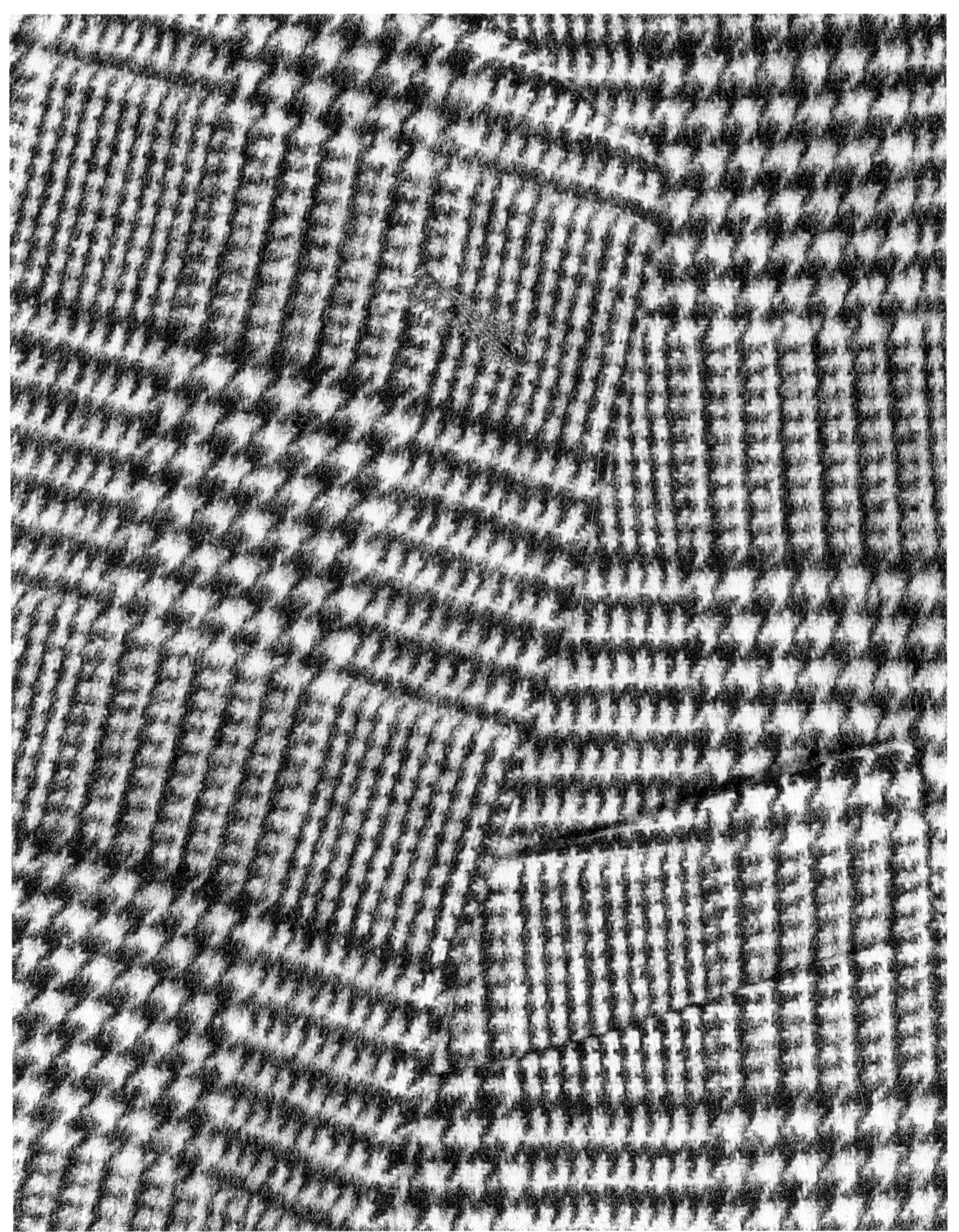

clockwise from top left The Stella Jean show at Milan Fashion Week autumn/winter 2015; a herringbone design by Joseph at London Fashion Week autumn/winter 2016; Vintage herringbone coat, Chicago 2016.

HERRINGBONE

THE TRADITIONAL TWEED

The herringbone pattern is a twill design constructed from columns of slanted lines to create a v-shape or zigzag pattern, taking its name from its similarity to the skeleton of a herring fish. The herringbone design was popular in the Outer Hebrides as a twill technique and is one of the most common patterns for Harris Tweed products. It can be manufactured in a wide range of colours, but the most popular is in shades of grey and black. The herringbone design can be given an overcheck to create an estate tweed, or with bird's-eye, coloured flecks throughout.[1]

It has been a popular design for men's suits and overcoats since the nineteenth century, in heavy or lightweight fabric, depending on how the item will be worn, and the darker tones of the herringbone made it more suitable for city living than checked designs. During the Second World War, herringbone tweed became a practical fabric for women's suits as it was hardwearing and could be adapted from men's old suits.

Since the 1970s, when he revived Ivy League fashions, Ralph Lauren often used the herringbone pattern for tweed jackets and coats for men and women. In the twenty-first century, herringbone tweeds have been adopted by hipsters and 'the young fogeys', with their interest in referencing old-fashioned British style.

left The Lena Hoschek show at the Mercedes-Benz Fashion Week in Berlin, 2016; ***right*** A 1991 fashion shoot with Emporio Armani tweed jacket and Ralph Lauren hat.

GUN CLUB

THE AMERICAN TWEED

The gun club check is also known as the Coigach Estate tweed, which is believed to date back to 1847. In 1870 the Coigach tweed was adopted by one of America's east coast gun clubs, either New York or Baltimore, possibly because of its camouflage colours. These were prestigious clubs and so lent a sense of exclusivity to the design. The style was exported back to Britain from America, known as the gun club check in the fashion world, where it became a very popular style for jackets and hats, with its east coast fashionable status.[1]

This tweed is an adaptation of the border shepherd check, and features even checks of brown, grey and black, originally created from the natural colours of the sheep's wool. It was a simple check that has been adopted by many estates for their tweeds, and the design shares similarities with the ancient Falkirk Tartan weave, making it one of the oldest known checks.[2]

Its simplicity meant it worked as a practical woven fabric for shepherds on the Borders hills where it could be woven domestically, and it was later adopted in neighbouring Northumberland for pipers of the Northumberland Fusiliers. Sir Walter Scott is said to have made the check popular by wearing the working man's fabric in pairs of trews when in London, and this helped to drive up the popularity of Borders mills.[3]

clockwise from top left Yves Saint Laurent Ready to Wear autumn/winter 2011/2012 show at Paris Fashion Week; Burberry glen check coat, street style Chicago, 2016; Cary Grant wearing a glen check suit in *North by Northwest*.

GLEN CHECK

IVY LEAGUE TWEED

The glen check, consisting of small and large checks in a windowpane design, is considered one of the most stylish of tweed patterns, favoured by Savile Row tailors, ad men on Madison Avenue in the 1950s and by James Bond in several movie incarnations. In *North by Northwest*, Cary Grant wears a finely tailored suit in a grey glen check throughout the film and Jon Hamm as Don Draper also wears the glen check in *Mad Men*.

Glen check comes from Glenurquhart in Inverness-shire, where the Seafield family owned an estate. In 1840 Lady Caroline Seafield designed the large check pattern as the Seafield's Glenurquhart estate tweed. Lady Caroline is believed to have been a weaver, but the Tartan Register of Scotland notes that it was likely woven by Elizabeth Macdougall of Lewston, at the foot of the glen.[1]

The check is also known as the Prince of Wales check; however this should describe a red, brown and white tweed rather than the grey, blue and white of the glen check. While it is often thought that it takes its name from Edward VIII (the Duke of Windsor after his abdication), it was named for his grandfather, Edward VII, Prince of Wales, who regularly took part in shooting expeditions on the Seafield estate, and who liked the check so much that he adopted it for himself.[2]

Edward VIII, as a trendsetter, made the glen check extremely popular in the 1930s and 1940s, and it was often the fabric of choice for fashionable jazz musicians and on university campuses such as Princeton. This in turn led to its popularity on Madison Avenue, where the fashion was heavily influenced by the cool jazz and Ivy League style.

clockwise from top left 1964 fashion shoot at Virginia Intermont College; actress Genevieve Bujold in 1966; Louis Verdad at Mercedes-Benz Fashion Week in 2006; Lauren Bacall with Humphrey Bogart in *To Have and Have Not* (1944).

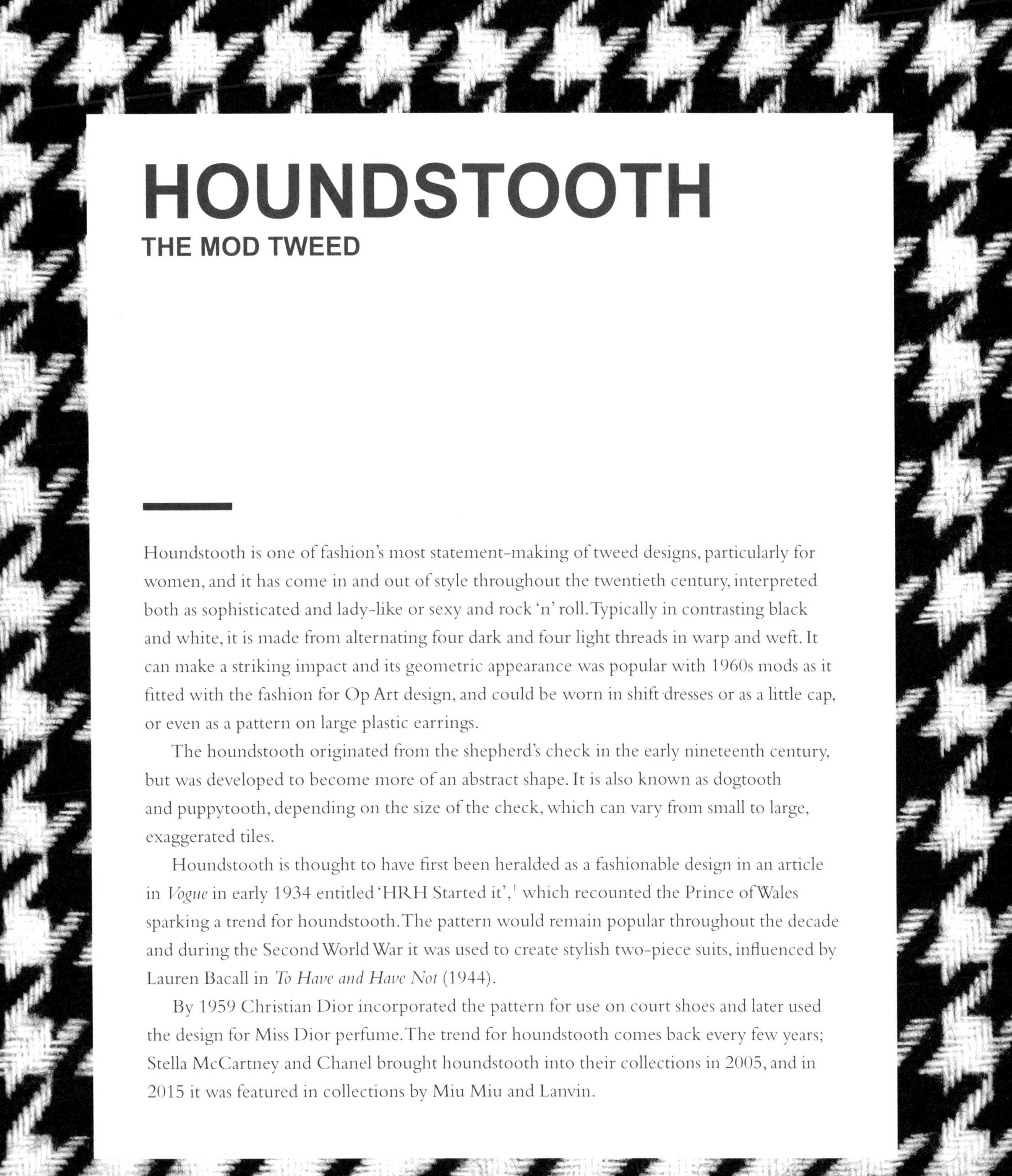

HOUNDSTOOTH

THE MOD TWEED

Houndstooth is one of fashion's most statement-making of tweed designs, particularly for women, and it has come in and out of style throughout the twentieth century, interpreted both as sophisticated and lady-like or sexy and rock 'n' roll. Typically in contrasting black and white, it is made from alternating four dark and four light threads in warp and weft. It can make a striking impact and its geometric appearance was popular with 1960s mods as it fitted with the fashion for Op Art design, and could be worn in shift dresses or as a little cap, or even as a pattern on large plastic earrings.

The houndstooth originated from the shepherd's check in the early nineteenth century, but was developed to become more of an abstract shape. It is also known as dogtooth and puppytooth, depending on the size of the check, which can vary from small to large, exaggerated tiles.

Houndstooth is thought to have first been heralded as a fashionable design in an article in *Vogue* in early 1934 entitled 'HRH Started it',[1] which recounted the Prince of Wales sparking a trend for houndstooth. The pattern would remain popular throughout the decade and during the Second World War it was used to create stylish two-piece suits, influenced by Lauren Bacall in *To Have and Have Not* (1944).

By 1959 Christian Dior incorporated the pattern for use on court shoes and later used the design for Miss Dior perfume. The trend for houndstooth comes back every few years; Stella McCartney and Chanel brought houndstooth into their collections in 2005, and in 2015 it was featured in collections by Miu Miu and Lanvin.

ENDNOTES

THE STORY OF TARTAN

1 Jonathan Faiers, *Tartan*, Berg Publishers, 2013, page 14.

2 *Colours of Hallstatt: Textiles Connecting Science and Art*, Natural History Museum Vienna, 2012.

3 National Museum of Scotland archives.

4 Virgil, *Aeneid*, Book VIII, cited in the Tartans Authority's tartan timeline. www.tartansauthority.com

5 I.F. Grant, *Highland Folk Ways*, Routledge & Kegan Paul, 1995, page 316.

6 Edward Burt, *Letters from a Gentleman in the North of Scotland to His Friend in London*, Ogle, Duncan & Co., 1822.

7 Culloden visitors centre, exhibition.

8 Burt, *Letters from a Gentleman*.

9 Ibid.

10 Cited in the Tartans Authority's tartan timeline. www.tartansauthority.com

11 Faiers, *Tartan*.

12 Ibid.

13 Professor Hugh Cheape interview, 22 March 2016.

14 James D. Scarlett, *Tartan: The Highland Textile*, Shepheard-Walwyn, 1990, page 45.

15 Faiers, *Tartan*, page 25.

16 J. Telfer Dunbar, *The Costumes of Scotland*, Batsford, 1981.

17 Hugh Cheape & Anita Quye, *Report on National Museum of Scotland Dye-Analysis Project Submitted as Evidence to the Economy, Energy & Tourist Committee of the Scottish Parliament*, April 2008.

18 Grant, *Highland Folk Ways*, page 333.

19 Ibid., pages 332–3.

20 Ibid., pages 326–9.

21 Frank Adam, *The Clans, Septs and Regiments of the Scottish Highlands*, Clearfield, 8th edn, 1999, page 371.

22 Grant, *Highland Folk Ways*, page 325.

23 Ian Brown (ed.), *From Tartan to Tartanry: Scottish Culture, History and Myth*, Edinburgh University Press, 2010, page 20.

24 Hugh Cheape, *Tartan: The Highland Habit*, NMSE Publishing, Edinburgh, 1995.

25 Sally Tuckett, 'Redressing the Romance: Tartan as a Popular Commodity, *c.*1770–1830', *Scottish Historical Review*, 2016.

26 Ibid.

27 Brown, *From Tartan to Tartanry*.

28 Cheape interview.

29 Ibid.

30 Ibid.

31 Ibid.

32 Tuckett, 'Redressing the Romance'.

33 R.R. McIan, *McIan's The Clans of the Scottish Highlands*, Pan Books, 1980.

34 Dunbar, *The Costumes of Scotland*.

35 Caroline de Guitaut, interview with curator of *Fashioning a Reign*, at the Palace of Holyrood House, Edinburgh, 22 April 2016.

36 Inverness Museum and Art Gallery, references.

THE HISTORY OF THE KILT

1 Stuart Reid, *Scottish National Dress and Tartan*, Shire Publications, 2013, page 31.

2 J. Telfer Dunbar, *Highland Costume*, William Blackwood & Sons, 1977, page 1.

3 Reid, *Scottish National Dress and Tartan*, page 41.

4 J. Andrew Henderson, *The Emperor's New Kilt*, Mainstream Publishing, 2000, page 79.

5 R.M.D. Grange, *A Short History of Highland Dress*, Burke's Peerage Ltd, 1966, page 60.

6 Hugh Trevor-Roper, *The Invention of Scotland*, Yale University Press, page 197.

7 Ibid., page 200.

8 Nick Fiddes, interview with owner of DC Dalgliesh, 11 July 2016.

9 William Mosman, 'John Campbell of the Bank', oil on canvas painting, National Gallery of Scotland. www.nationalgalleries.org

10 Robin Nicholson, 'From Ramsay's *Flora MacDonald* to Raeburn's *MacNab*: The Use of Tartan as a Symbol of Identity', *Textile History*, Vol. 36, No. 2, 2005.

11 Trevor-Roper, *The Invention of Scotland*, page 192.

MYTHS OF TARTAN

1 Samuel Johnson & Arthur Murphy, *The Works of Samuel Johnson*, printed by Thomas Davison, Whitefriars, 1824, page 429.

2 Jonathan Faiers, *Tartan*, Berg Publishers, 2013, page 243.

3 Colin McArthur, *Brigadoon, Braveheart and the Scots: Distortion of Scotland in Hollywood Cinema*, Taurus & Co., 2003.

4 Ibid.

5 Ibid., page 110.

6 Ibid.

7 Queen Victoria, *Leaves from the Journal of Our Life in the Highlands, from 1848 to 1861*, edited by Arthur Helps, The Folio Society, London, 1973.

8 Ibid.

9 R.R. McIan, *McIan's The Clans of the Scottish Highlands*, Pan Books, 1980.

10 Andrew Bolton, *Anglomania: Tradition and Transgression in British Fashion*, Metropolitan Museum of Art Publications, 2007, page 51.

11 Allan Massie, *The Royal Stuarts: A History of the Family that Shaped Britain*, Jonathan Cape, 2010, page 153.

12 Sharon L. Krossa, *Braveheart Errors*. Retrieved from www.medievalscotland.org

13 Mel Gibson, '"*Braveheart* Wallace is a Monster", Says Gibson', *The Scotsman*, 24 October 2009.

14 Lucinda Lax, interview with senior curator, Scottish National Portrait Gallery, Edinburgh, 22 March 2016.

15 Scottish National Portrait Gallery, Edinburgh, Jacobite collection.

16 Ibid.

17 Ibid.

18 McIan, *McIan's The Clans of the Scottish Highlands*.

19 *New York Times*, 'Some Words about Sir Walter Scott', 17 September 1871.

20 British *Vogue*, 'Louis Vuitton Autumn/Winter 2004–2005', 8 March 2004.

21 Visit Scotland, '*Brave* Marketing Opportunity'. www.visitscotland.org

THE POPULARITY OF TARTAN

1 Richard Blaustein, *The Thistle and the Brier*, McFarland & Co., 2003, page 73.

2 Alice Fisher, 'Why the World Has Gone Mad for Plaid', *The Observer*, 11 April 2010.

3 Jonathan Faiers, *Tartan*, Berg Publishers, 2013.

4 Zoe Heller, 'Hollywood gets ready for the crazy, sexy charm of Ewan McGregor', *Vanity Fair*, December 1998.

5 Ian Brown (ed.), *From Tartan to Tartanry: Scottish Culture, History and Myth*, Edinburgh University Press, 2010.

6 Fiona Ritchie & Doug Orr, *Wayfaring Strangers: The Musical Voyage from Scotland and Ulster to Appalachia*, The University of North Carolina Press, 2014.

7 Ian Maitland Hume, in Ian Brown (ed.), *From Tartan to Tartanry: Scottish Culture, History and Myth*, Edinburgh University Press, 2010, page 68.

8 Ritchie & Orr, *Wayfaring Strangers*.

9 Melissa Ruggieri, 'John Fogerty Talks Flannel Shirts', *Access Atlanta*, 15 October 2013.

10 *Toronto Sun*, 'John Fogerty Relives 1960 in Cross Canada Tour', 11 September 2014.

11 Woolrich, *The History of Woolrich. The Original Outdoor Clothing Company*. www.woolrich.com

12 Pendleton, *Company History*. www.pendleton-usa.com

13 Bruce G. Boyer, *Ivy Style: Radical Conformists*, Yale University Press, Fashion Institute of Technology, 2012.

14 Victoria & Albert Museum, collections.

15 Virginia Pope, 'Plaid Popularity', *New York Times*, 10 July 1949.

16 Paul Maloney, in Ian Brown (ed.), *From Tartan to Tartanry: Scottish Culture, History and Myth*, Edinburgh University Press, 2010, page 135.

17 Colin McArthur, *Brigadoon, Braveheart and the Scots: Distortion of Scotland in Hollywood Cinema*, Taurus & Co., 2003.

18 Penny Valentine, 'Swashbuckler Rod', *Sounds* magazine, August 1973.

19 Steven Brocklehurst, 'Bay City Rollers: The Boy Band that Turned the World Tartan', *The Times*, 13 September 2015.

20 Michael Leapman, 'Diary', *The Times*, 5 December 1975.

21 Chris Brown, *Booted and Suited*, John Blake, 2009.

22 Vivienne Westwood & Ian Kelly, *Vivienne Westwood*, Pan Macmillan, 2014, Kindle edn location 2306.

23 Andrew Bolton, *Punk: Chaos to Couture*, Yale University Press, 2013.

24 Ibid.

25 Madonna, *Interview* magazine, March 2001.

26 *The Guardian*, 'Brigadoon is Alive with the Sound of Money', 18 December 2000.

27 *The Face*, 'Grunge Fashion', August 1992.

28 Nancy Miller, *Breathless: An American Girl in Paris*, Seal Press, 2013, page 221.

29 Valerie Steele, Patricia Mears, Yuniya Kawamuram & Hiroshi Narushi, *Japan Fashion Now*, Fashion Institute of Technology, Yale University Press, 2010, page 28.

30 Elissa Strauss, '*Clueless* Designer Mona May Didn't Want Cher to Look Over-Sexed', *Elle*, 15 July 2015.

31 Steven Daly, 'Inside the Heart and Mind and Bedroom of America's New Teen Queen', *Rolling Stone*, April 1999.

32 *The Telegraph*, 'Bravo for Burberry', 9 July 2000.

TARTAN IN STREET STYLE

1 Daniele Bott, *Chanel: Collections and Creations*, Thames & Hudson, 2007.

2 Claire Wilcox, *Vivienne Westwood*, V&A Publishing, 2004, page 15.

3 Colin McDowell, *The Man of Fashion: Peacock Males and Perfect Gentlemen*, Thames & Hudson, 1997, page 98.

4 Tommy Hilfiger & David A. Keeps, *All American: A Style Book*, Pavilion, 1998, page 39.

5 Alice Fisher, 'Why the World Has Gone Mad for Plaid', *The Guardian*, 11 April 2010.

6 Gordon Millar, interview with founder of Scot Street Style, 26 April 2016.

7 James Bent, *Asian Street Fashion*, Thames & Hudson, 2014, page 68.

TARTAN IN CONTEMPORARY FASHION

1 Linda Watson, *Vogue on Westwood*, Quadrille, 2003.

2 Linda Watson, *Twentieth-Century Fashion*, Carlton Books, 1999, page 63.

3 Catherine McDermott & Edwina Ehram, *Vivienne Westwood: A London Fashion*, Philip Wilson Publishers, 2000, page 22.

4 Alexander McQueen, 'Cutting Up Rough', *The Works*, series 3, episode 9, BBC television documentary, July 1997.

5 Alexander McQueen, interview with *The Independent Fashion Magazine*, *Savage Beauty* exhibition. www.metmuseum.org

6 Kate Bethune, interview with curator at Victoria & Albert Museum, March 2016.

7 Alexander McQueen, *Time Out*, London, 24 September–1 October 1997.

8 Andrew Wilson, *Alexander McQueen: Blood Beneath the Skin*, Simon & Schuster, 2015, page 138.

9 James Bent, *Asian Street Fashion*, Thames & Hudson, 2014, page 12.

10 Colin McDowell, *Ralph Lauren: The Man, The Vision, The Style*, Cassell Illustrated, 2002, page 61.

11 Watson, *Twentieth-Century Fashion*, page 286.

12 Antony Shugaar, 'The Comedy of Errors: Gender Icons as Modular Components of Identity', in Giannino Malossi (ed.), *Material Man: Masculinity Sexuality Style*, Harry N. Abrams Publishers, 2000, page 67.

13 Jeffrey Banks & Doria de la Chapelle, *Tartan: Romancing the Plaid*, Rizzoli, 2015, page 128.

14 Thierry-Maxime Loriot, *The Fashion World of Jean Paul Gaultier*, Editions de la Martinière, 2001, page 214.

15 Andrew Bolton, *Punk: Chaos to Couture*, Yale University Press, 2013, page 105.

16 Tommy Hilfiger & David A. Keeps, *All American: A Style Book*, Pavilion, 1998. Page 152.

17 Isaac Mizrahi, 'Isaac Mizrahi on Tartan', part of 'Isaac Mizrahi: An Unruly History', Jewish Museum Sound Cloud recording, 18 March–7 August 2016. www.thejewishmuseum.org

18 Samantha McCoach, interview with founder of Le Kilt, 27 April 2016.

THE ORIGINS OF TWEED

1 Douglas Fraser, 'Harris Tweed: Weaving a Brighter Future', *BBC News*, 8 June 2013. www.bbc.co.uk

2 Lorna Macaulay, interview with chief executive, Harris Tweed Authority, 7 March 2016.

3 Janet Hunter, *The Islanders and the Orb: The History of the Harris Tweed Industry*, Acair Books, 2001, page 71.

THE FALL + RISE OF HARRIS TWEED

1 Janet Hunter, *The Islanders and the Orb: The History of the Harris Tweed Industry*, Acair Books, 2001, page 132.

2 Andy Pike, *Origination: The Geographies of Brands and Branding*, John Wiley, 2015, page 191.

3 Development Working Party Meeting Minutes in Hunter, *The Islanders and the Orb: The History of the Harris Tweed Industry*.

4 *Harris Tweed Information Pack 2014*, Harris Tweed Authority .

5 Lorna Macaulay, interview with chief executive of the Harris Tweed Authority, 7 March 2016.

6 Macauley interview.

7 Patrick Grant, interview with owner of E. Tautz, 3 May 2016.

COCO CHANEL IN SCOTLAND

1 Axel Madsen, *Coco Chanel: A Biography*, Bloomsbury, 2009, page 10.

2 Amy de la Haye, *Chanel*, V&A Publishing, 2011, page 16.

3 Madsen, *Coco Chanel*.

4 British *Vogue*, 'Chanel is Master of Her Art and Her Art Resides in Jersey', 1 November 1916.

5 Justine Picardie, *Coco Chanel: The Legend and The Life*, Harper, 2013.

6 Ibid.

7 *The Guardian*, 'Chanel Revives Franco-Scottish Love Affair in Tweedy Fashion', 4 December 2012.

8 *The Guardian*, 'Chanel Revives Franco-Scottish Love Affair in Tweedy Fashion'.

9 Patricia M. Hitchon, *Chanel and the Tweedmaker: Weaver of Dreams*, P3 Publications, September 2012.

10 Ibid.

11 Ibid.

12 *Vogue*, 'Scottish Tweed is a New Godchild of French Couturiers', October 1927.

TWEED IN CONTEMPORARY FASHION

1 Daniele Bott, *Chanel: Collections and Creations*, Thames & Hudson, 2007.

2 Patricia M. Hitchon, *Chanel and the Tweedmaker: Weavers of Dreams*, P3 Publications, 2012, page 218.

3 British *Vogue*, 'Chanel Autumn/Winter 2005 Ready To Wear', March 2005.

4 Karl Lagerfeld, 'The Jacket', *Inside Chanel* video. Retrieved from www.inside.chanel.com

5 Carmel Allen (ed.), *The Fashion Book*, Phaidon Press, London, 2014.

6 Terry Jones & Avril Mair (eds), *Fashion Now: i-D Selects the World's 150 Most Important Designers*, Taschen, 2003, page 331.

7 Hilary Alexander, '"I Do Like to See Aggression" Alexander McQueen Has a New Lease of Life', *Daily Telegraph*, 7 June 2001.

8 Judy R Clark, interview with founder of Judy R Clark, April 2016.

9 Press Association, 'Alexander McQueen: Savage Beauty Is Most Popular Show in V&A's History', *The Guardian*, 3 August 2015.

10 Vivienne Westwood & Ian Kelly, *Vivienne Westwood*, Picador, 2014, page 290.

11 Claire Wilcox, *Vivienne Westwood*, V&A Publishing, 2004, page 20.

12 Patrick Grant, interview with owner of E. Tautz, 3 May 2016.

13 Guy Hills, interview with founder of Dashing Tweeds, April 2016.

14 Ibid.

15 Ibid.

16 Ibid.

17 James Sherwood, *Savile Row: The Master Tailors of British Bespoke*, Thames & Hudson, 2010, page 212.

18 Hills interview.

19 Nigel Cabourn, interview with founder of Nigel Cabourn, July 2016.

20 Cabourn interview.

21 Ibid.

22 Scotland Office & The Rt Hon David Mundell MP, 'Harris Tweed Celebrates UK Revival at the Scotland Office', 23 February 2016. www.gov.uk

23 Interview with Margaret Howell, 23 August 2016.

24 Clark interview.

25 Ibid.

TWEED IN FASHION CULURES

1 *The Guardian*, 'CIA Agents Look Better in Harris Tweed', 9 April 2013.

2 Lady Anne Dunmore, interview with the current Countess of Dunmore, 10 April 2016.

3 Rational Dress Society, *The Rational Dress Society's Gazette*, January 1889.

4 Kathleen E. McCrone, *Playing the Game: Sport and the Physical Emancipation of English Women*, University Press of Kentucky, 1988.

5 *Punch*, Vol. 84, June 1883.

6 Steven McKenzie, 'The World-Wide Fascination in Sherlock Holmes' Tweed Cape', *BBC Online*, 5 November 2014.

7 *New York Times*, 'Tuberculosis Scare in London', 25 August 1901.

8 Bruce G. Boyer, *Ivy Style: Radical Conformists*, Yale University Press, Fashion Institute of Technology, 2012.

9 Ibid.

10 Peter York, 'The Fall of the Sloane Rangers', *Prospect Magazine*, 19 February 2015.

11 *New York Times*, 'On the Trail of London's Sloane Rangers', 25 March 1984.

12 Suzy Menkes, 'Men's Fashion by Suzy Menkes, A Touch of the Old Etonians', *The Times*, 5 October 1982.

13 Suzy Menkes, 'Younger Gentlemen Prefer Tweeds', *The Times*, 19 November 1985.

14 Clare Raymond, 'Country Wife', *Mirror*, 19 August 2005.

15 Viola Henderson, 'The Modern Sloane', *Tatler*, 25 March 2013.

16 Katherine Gleason, *Anatomy of Steampunk*, Race Point Publishing, 2013.

17 See www.tweedrun.com.

18 Paul Bignell, ' "What Ho!" Lay Out Your Best Tweeds – Chaps Are Dressing Up Again'. *Independent*, 23 April 2011.

TARTAN, TWEED + ROYALTY

1 Allan Massie, *The Royal Stuarts: A History of the Family that Shaped Britain*, Jonathan Cape, 2010, page 66.

2 Hugh Cheape, *Tartan, the Highland Habit*, NMSE Publishing, Edinburgh, 1995.

3 R.M.D. Grange, *A Short History of the Scottish Dress*, Macmillan, 1967, page 15.

4 National Records Scotland, Exchequer Records (Ref: E21/34).

5 Information on the watercolour portrait of Mary, Queen of Scots, *c.*1558, by François Clouet, The Royal Collection.

6 Massie, *The Royal Stuarts.*

7 Ibid.

8 R.R. McIan, *McIan's The Clans of the Scottish Highlands*, Pan Books, 1980.

9 *The Times*, report on George IV visit, 7 August 1822.

10 Colin W. Hutcheson, *Royal Tartans*. www.tartansauthority.com

11 Ian Mitchell, *On the Trail of Queen Victoria in the Highlands,* Luath Press, 2000, page 10.

12 A.N. Wilson, *Victoria: A Life*, Atlantic Books, 2014, page 141.

13 Kate Hubbard, *Serving Victoria: Life in the Royal Household*, Vintage, 2012.

14 Queen Victoria, *Leaves from the Journal of Our Life in the Highlands, from 1848 to 1861*, edited by Arthur Helps, The Folio Society, London, 1973.

15 C. Willett Cunnington, *English Women's Clothing in the Nineteenth Century,* Dover Publications, rev. edn 1990, page 21.

16 Ibid., pages 236, 263.

17 Mitchell, *On the Trail*, page 41.

18 Wilson, *Victoria*, page 225.

19 Clair Price, 'The Prince of Wales Fashion', *New York Times*, 27 October 1929.

20 Anne Sebba, *That Woman: The Life of the Duchess of Windsor*, Weidenfeld & Nicolson, 2012, page 74.

21 Ibid.

22 Anne Sebba, 'The Report: The Duke of Windsor', *Mr Porter: The Journal*, 6 September 2011.

23 Bruce G. Boyer, *Ivy Style: Radical Conformists*, Yale University Press, Fashion Institute of Technology, 2012.

24 Ibid.

25 Sebba, *That Woman.*

26 Patricia M. Hitchon, *Chanel and the Tweedmaker: Weaver of Dreams*, P3 Publications, September 2012.

27 Caroline de Guitaut, interview with curator of *Fashioning a Reign*, at the Palace of Holyrood House, Edinburgh, 20 April 2016.

28 William Shawcross, *Queen Elizabeth: The Queen Mother*, Macmillan, 2009, page 799.

29 Catherine Ostler, 'Nostalgia: The Queen's Changing Fashion', *Vogue*, 1 June 2012.

30 De Guitaut interview.

31 Tina Brown, *Diana Chronicles*, Random House, 2007, page 144.

32 Ibid., page 145.

33 Georgina Howell, *Diana: Her Life in Fashion*, Rizzoli, 1998.

34 De Guitaut interview.

A BUYER'S GUIDE TO TARTAN

1 Peter Macdonald, 'The Use of Colour in Tartan', page 2. www.scottishtartans.co.uk

2 Scottish Tartans Authority, 'Matthew Newsome'. www.tartansauthority.com

3 The Scottish Register of Tartans, 'Tartan Details – Fraser' (1745). www.tartanregister.gov.uk

4 Charles J. Thompson, *So You're Going to Wear the Kilt: All You Want to Know about Tartan Dress*, Lang Syne Publishers, 3rd edn 1989.

5 Ibid.

BLACKWATCH

1 William Scobie, 'Black Watch', Scottish Tartans Authority. www.tartansauthority.com

2 Singer, Maya, 'McQ Alexander McQueen review', *Vogue*, 20 February 2012.

MACLEOD

1 The Scottish Register of Tartans, 'Tartan Details - MacLeod of Lewis (Vestiarium Scoticum)'. www.tartanregister.gov.uk

STEWART

1 British *Vogue*, 'D & G autumn/winter 2008', 18 February 2008.

A BUYER'S GUIDE TO TWEED

1 Lara Platman, *Harris Tweed: From Land to Street*, Frances Lincoln, 2014.

2 E.P. Harrison, *Scottish Estate Tweeds*, Johnstons of Elgin, 1995, page 11.

3 Paul Walker, interview with founder of Walker Slater, Edinburgh, 1 April 2016.

GUN CLUB

1 E.P. Harrison, *Scottish Estate Tweeds*, Johnstons of Elgin, 1995, page 26.

2 The Scottish Register of Tartans, 'Tartan Display: Shepherd Check Universal'. www.tartansauthority.com

3 The Northumberland Tartan Company, 'History'. www.northumberlandtartan.co.uk

GLEN CHECK

1 The Scottish Register of Tartans, 'Tartan Details - Glenurquhart Estate Check'. www.tartanregister.gov.uk

2 *Esquire magazine*, 'The Bespokeman – Glen Check Fabric', 3 August 2009.

HOUNDSTOOTH

1 *Vogue*, 'HRH Started It', 15 January 1934.

HERRINGBONE

1 Paul Walker, interview with founder of Walker Slater, Edinburgh, 1 April 2016.

SELECT BIBLIOGRAPHY

Adam, Frank, *The Clans, Septs and Regiments of the Scottish Highlands*, Clearfield, 8th edn, 1999.

Ahrendts, Angela, 'Burberry's CEO on Turning an Aging British Icon into a Global Luxury Brand', *Harvard Business Review*, January–February 2013.

Alexander, Hilary, '"I Do Like to See Aggression" Alexander McQueen Has a New Lease of Life', *Daily Telegraph*, 7 June 2001.

Allen, Carmel (ed.), *The Fashion Book*, Phaidon Press, 2014.

Angus Macleod Archive. www.angusmacleodarchive.org.uk

Banks, Jeffrey & Chapelle, Doria de la, *Tartan: Romancing the Plaid*, Rizzoli, 2015.

BBC News, 'Burberry's Journey Through Fashion', 29 May 2002.

Bent, James, *Asian Street Fashion*, Thames & Hudson, 2014.

Bignell, Paul, '"What Ho!" Lay Out Your Best Tweeds – Chaps Are Dressing Up Again'. *Independent*, 23 April 2011.

Blaustein, Richard, *The Thistle and the Brier*, McFarland & Co., 2003.

Bolton, Andrew, *Anglomania: Tradition and Transgression in British Fashion*, Metropolitan Museum of Art Publications, 2007.

Bolton, Andrew, *Punk: Chaos to Couture*, Yale University Press, 2013.

Bothwell, Claire, 'Shoemaker Nike's Fling with Harris Tweed', *BBC News*, 19 October 2004.

Bott, Daniele, *Chanel: Collections and Creations*, Thames & Hudson, 2007.

Boyer, Bruce G., *Ivy Style: Radical Conformists*, Yale University Press, Fashion Institute of Technology, 2012.

Breward, Christopher, Ehrman, Edwina & Edwards, Caroline, *The London Look: Fashion from Street to Catwalk*, Yale University Press, 2004.

British Vogue, 'Chanel is Master of Her Art and Her Art Resides in Jersey', 1 November 1916.

British *Vogue*, 'D & G autumn/winter 2008', 18 February 2008.

British Vogue, 'Louis Vuitton Autumn/Winter 2004-2005', 8 March 2004.

British Vogue, March 2005[please supply details here and in note 3]

Brocklehurst, Steven, 'Bay City Rollers: The Boy Band that Turned the World Tartan', *The Times*, 13 September 2015.

Brown, Chris, *Booted and Suited*, John Blake, 2009.

Brown, Ian (ed.), *From Tartan to Tartanry: Scottish Culture, History and Myth*, Edinburgh University Press, 2010.

Brown, Tina, *Diana Chronicles*, Random House, 2007.

Burt, Edward, *Letters from a Gentleman in the North of Scotland to His Friend in London*, Ogle, Duncan & Co., 1822.

Cabourn, Nigel, interview with founder of Nigel Cabourn, July 2016.

Cheape, Hugh, *Tartan: The Highland Habit*, NMSE Publishing, Edinburgh, 1995.

Cheape, Hugh & Quye, Anita, *Report on National Museum of Scotland Dye-Analysis Project Submitted as Evidence to the Economy, Energy & Tourist Committee of the Scottish Parliament*, April 2008.

Cochrane, Lauren, 'Chanel's Little Black Jacket: How Lagerfeld Reinvented Tweed', *The Guardian*, 12 October 2012.

Colours of Hallstatt: Textiles Connecting Science and Art, Natural History Museum Vienna, 2012.

Cowing, Emma, 'Origins of Chanel Jacket Are Scottish', *Scotsman*, 6 October 2013.

Cunnington, C. Willett, *English Women's Clothing in the Nineteenth Century*, Dover Publications, rev. edn 1990.

Daly, Steven, 'Inside the Heart and Mind and Bedroom of America's New Teen Queen', *Rolling Stone*, April 1999.

De la Haye, Amy, *Chanel*, V&A Publishing, 2011.

Dunbar, J. Telfer, *Highland Costume*, William Blackwood & Sons, 1977.

Dunbar, J. Telfer, *The Costumes of Scotland*, Batsford, 1981.

Esquire magazine, 'The Bespokeman – Glen Check Fabric', 3 August 2009

Faiers, Jonathan, *Tartan*, Berg Publishers, 2013.

Fisher, Alice, 'Why the World Has Gone Mad for Plaid', *The Observer*, 11 April 2010.

Fox, Chloe, *Vogue on Alexander McQueen*, Quadrille, 2012.

Fraser, Douglas, 'Harris Tweed: Weaving a Brighter Future', *BBC News*, 8 June 2013.

Fulton, Alexander, *Scotland and Her Tartans: The Romantic Heritage of Clans and Families*, Hodder & Stoughton, London, 1991.

Gibson, Mel, '"*Braveheart* Wallace Is a Monster", Says Gibson', *The Scotsman*, 24 October 2009.

Gleason, Katherine, *Anatomy of Steampunk*, Race Point Publishing, 2013.

Grange, R.M.D., *A Short History of Highland Dress*, Burke's Peerage Ltd, 1966.

Grange, R.M.D., *A Short History of the Scottish Dress*, Macmillan, 1967.

Grant, I.F., *Highland Folk Ways*, Routledge & Kegan Paul, 1995.

Grant, James, *The Clans and Tartans of Scotland*, Wordsworth Editions, 1992.

Grayson, Richard, *Tartan Conspiracy*, Macmillan, 1992.

Harkins, Anthony, *Hillbilly: A Cultural History of an American Icon*, Oxford University Press.

www.harristweed.org

Heller, Zoe, 'Hollywood Gets Ready For the Crazy, Sexy Charm of Ewan McGregor', *Vanity Fair*, December 1998.

Henderson, J. Andrew, *The Emperor's New Kilt*, Mainstream Publishing, 2000.

Henderson, Viola, 'The Modern Sloane', *Tatler*, 25 March 2013.

Hilfiger, Tommy & Keeps, David A., *All American: A Style Book*, Pavilion, 1998.

Hitchon, Patricia M., *Chanel and the Tweedmaker: Weaver of Dreams*, P3 Publications, September 2012.

Howell, Georgina, *Diana: Her Life in Fashion*, Rizzoli, 1998.

Hubbard, Kate, *Serving Victoria: Life in the Royal Household*, Vintage, 2012.

Hunter, Janet, *The Islanders and the Orb: The History of the Harris Tweed Industry*, Acair Books, 2001.

Johnson, Samuel & Murphy, Arthur, *The Works of Samuel Johnson*, printed by Thomas Davison, Whitefriars, 1824.

Johnstons of Elgin, *Scottish Estate Tweeds*, 1995.

Jones, Terry & Mair, Avril (eds), *Fashion Now: i-D Selects the World's 150 Most Important Designers*, Taschen, 2003.

Kinloch Anderson, Deirdre, *A Scottish Tradition: Tailors and Kilt-Makers, Tartan and Highland Dress since 1868*, Neil Wilson Publishing, 2013.

Lawson, Ian, *From the Land Comes the Cloth: Harris Tweed*, Ian Lawson Books, 2011.

Leapman, Michael, 'Diary', *The Times*, 5 December 1975.

Loriot, Thierry-Maxime, *The Fashion World of Jean Paul Gaultier*, Editions de la Martinière, 2001.

Madsen, Axel, *Coco Chanel: A Biography*, Bloomsbury, 2009.

Martin, Richard, *Jocks and Nerds: Men's Style in the Twentieth Century*, Rizzoli, 1989.

Massie, Allan, *The Royal Stuarts: A History of the Family that Shaped Britain*, Jonathan Cape, 2010.

McArthur, Colin, *Brigadoon, Braveheart and the Scots: Distortion of Scotland in Hollywood Cinema*, Taurus & Co., 2003.

McCrone, Kathleen E., *Playing the Game: Sport and the Physical Emancipation of English Women*, University Press of Kentucky, 1988.

McDermott, Catherine & Ehram, Edwina, *Vivienne Westwood: A London Fashion*, Philip Wilson Publishers, 2000.

McDowell, Colin, *The Man of Fashion: Peacock Males and Perfect Gentlemen*, Thames & Hudson, 1997.

McDowell, Colin, *Ralph Lauren: The Man, The Vision, The Style*, Cassell Illustrated, 2002.

McIan, R.R. & Logan, James, *McIan's The Clans of the Scottish Highlands*, Pan Books, 1980.

McKenzie, Steven, 'The World-Wide Fascination in Sherlock Holmes' Tweed Cape', *BBC Online*, 5 November 2014.

McOwan, Rennie, *Tartans: The Facts and Myths*, Jarrold Publishing, 1990.

Menkes, Suzy, 'Men's Fashion by Suzy Menkes, A Touch of the Old Etonians', *The Times*, 5 October 1982.

Menkes, Suzy, 'Younger Gentlemen Prefer Tweeds', *The Times*, 19 November 1985.

Miller, Nancy, *Breathless: An American Girl in Paris*, Seal Press, 2013.

Mitchell, Ian, *On the Trail of Queen Victoria in the Highlands*, Luath Press, 2000.

Nemy, Enid, 'Tartans: A Current Fashion with a Long History', *New York Times*, 6 December 1971.

New York Times, 'On the Trail of London's Sloane Rangers', 25 March 1984.

New York Times, 'Some Words about Sir Walter Scott', 17 September 1871.

New York Times, 'Tuberculosis Scare in London', 25 August 1901.

Nicholson, Robin, 'From Ramsay's *Flora MacDonald* to Raeburn's *MacNab*: The Use of Tartan as a Symbol of Identity', Textile *History*, Vol. 36, No. 2, 2005.

Ostler, Catherine, 'Nostalgia: The Queen's Changing Fashion', *Vogue*, 1 June 2012.

Pearlman, Chee, Lehmann, Ulrich, Taxter, Kelly & Yaeger, Lynn, *Isaac Mizrahi*, Yale University Press, 2016.

Picardie, Justine, *Coco Chanel: The Legend and the Life*, Harper, 2013.

Pike, Andy, *Origination: The Geographies of Brands and Branding*, John Wiley, 2015.

Pirnie, David B. (ed.), *The Big Cloth: The History and Making of Harris Tweed*, Highland Craftpoint, Inverness, 1981.

Platman, Lara, *Harris Tweed: From Land to Street*, Frances Lincoln, 2014.

Pope, Virginia, 'Plaid Popularity', *New York Times*, 10 July 1949.

Price, Clair, 'The Prince of Wales Fashion', *New York Times*, 27 October 1929.

Punch, Vol. 84, June 1883.

Queen Victoria, *Leaves from the Journal of Our Life in the Highlands, from 1848 to 1861*, edited by Arthur Helps, The Folio Society, London, 1973.

Rational Dress Society, *The Rational Dress Society's Gazette*, January 1889.

Raymond, Clare, 'Country Wife', *Mirror*, 19 August 2005.

Reid, Stuart, *Scottish National Dress and Tartan*, Shire Publications, 2013.

Ritchie, Fiona and Orr, Doug, *Wayfaring Strangers: The Musical Voyage from Scotland and Ulster to Appalachia*, The University of North Carolina Press, 2014.

Royce-Greensill, Sarah, 'The Making of Chanel Tweed', *The Telegraph*, 22 November 2014.

Royle, Trevor, *The Gordon Highlanders: A Concise History*, Random House, 2011.

Ruggieri, Melissa, 'John Fogerty Talks Flannel Shirts', *Access Atlanta*, 15 October 2013.

Scarlett, James D., *Tartan: The Highland Textile*, Shepheard-Walwyn, 1990.

Sebba, Anne, *That Woman: The Life of the Duchess of Windsor*, Weidenfeld & Nicolson, 2012.

Sebba, Anne, 'The Report: The Duke of Windsor', *Mr Porter: The Journal*, 6 September 2011.

Shawcross, William, *Queen Elizabeth: The Queen Mother*, Macmillan, 2009.

Sherwood, James, *Savile Row: The Master Tailors of British Bespoke*, Thames & Hudson, 2010.

Shugaar, Antony, 'The Comedy of Errors: Gender Icons as Modular Components of

Identity', in Giannino Malossi (ed.), *Material Man: Masculinity Sexuality Style*, Harry N. Abrams Publishers, 2000.

Singer, Maya, 'McQ Alexander McQueen review', *Vogue*, 20 February 2012.

Steele, Valerie, Mears, Patricia, Kawamuram, Yuniya & Narushi, Hiroshi, *Japan Fashion Now*, Fashion Institute of Technology, Yale University Press, 2010.

The Economist, 'A Checkered Story', 20 January 2011.

The Face, 'Grunge Fashion', August 1992.

The Guardian, 'Brigadoon Is Alive with the Sound of Money', 18 December 2000.

The Guardian, 'Chanel Revives Franco-Scottish Love Affair in Tweedy Fashion', 4 December 2012.

The Guardian, 'CIA Agents Look Better in Harris Tweed', 9 April 2013.

www.tartansauthority.com

www.tartanregister.gov.uk

The Telegraph, 'Bravo for Burberry', 9 July 2000.

The Times, report on George IV visit, 7 August 1822.

Thomas, Dana, *Gods and Kings: The Rise and Fall of Alexander McQueen and John Galliano*, Penguin, 2015.

Thompson, Charles J., *So You're Going to Wear the Kilt: All You Want to Know about Tartan Dress*, Lang Syne Publishers, 3rd edn 1989.

Thompson, Francis, *Harris Tweed: The Story of a Hebridean Industry*, David & Charles, 1969.

Toomey, Philippa, 'Shopping', *The Times*, 5 October 1976.

Toronto Sun, 'John Fogerty Relives 1960 in Cross Canada Tour', 11 September 2014.

Trevor-Roper, Hugh, *The Invention of Scotland*, Yale University Press.

Tuckett, Sally, interview with lecturer in History of Dress and Textiles (History of Art), Glasgow University, 8 April 2016.

Tuckett, Sally, 'Redressing the Romance: Tartan as a Popular Commodity, *c.*1770–1830', *Scottish Historical Review*, 2016.

V, Lorna, 'All Hail McQueen', *Time Out*, London, 24 September–1 October 1997.

Valentine, Penny, 'Swashbuckler Rod', *Sounds* magazine, August 1973.

Vogue, October 1927 [Article name?]

Vogue, 'HRH Started It', 15 January 1934

Walker, Rob, 'The Good, the Plaid and the Ugly', *New York Times*, 2 January 2005.

Waplington, Nick, *Alexander McQueen: Working Process*, Damiani, 2013.

Watson, Linda, *Twentieth-Century Fashion*, Carlton Books, 1999.

Watson, Linda, *Vogue on Westwood*, Quadrille, 2003.

Westwood, Vivienne & Kelly, Ian, *Vivienne Westwood*, Picador, 2014.

Wilcox, Claire, *Alexander McQueen*, V&A Publishing, 2015.

Wilcox, Claire, *Vivienne Westwood*, V&A Publishing, 2004.

Wilson, A.N., *Victoria: A Life*, Atlantic Books, 2014.

Wilson, Andrew, *Alexander McQueen: Blood Beneath the Skin*, Simon & Schuster, 2015.

Wilton, Brian, *Tartans*, The National Trust for Scotland, 2007.

York, Peter, 'The Fall of the Sloane Rangers', *Prospect Magazine*, 19 February 2015.

Yotka, Steff, 'Karl Lagerfeld's Most Memorable Twists on the Chanel Suit', *Vogue*, 7 March 2016.

Zaczek, Ian & Phillips, Charles, *The Illustrated Encyclopedia of Tartan*, Anness Publishing, 2013.

INDEX

PICTURE CREDITS

Courtesy Academy of Motion Picture Arts and Sciences: 43

akg-images: 41 top (Sotheby's)

Bridgeman Images: 23 (Private Collection/ photo © Agnew's, London), 46 left (Private Collection/photo © Philip Mould Ltd, London), 50 (Scottish National Gallery, Edinburgh)

Courtesy Judy R Clark, judyrclark.com: 152 top left (David Stanton, www.stantonimaging.co.uk)

Courtesy Dashing Tweeds, www.dashingtweeds.co.uk: 149 top, 150 top, 150 bottom

Getty Images: 15 (Hulton Archive), 16 left (Florilegius/SSPL), 19 right (James Valentine/Sean Sexton/Hulton Archive), 20 (Roger Fenton), 21 (SSPL), 24 (Keystone Features), 27 top & bottom (SSPL), 28 (Print Collector), 33 (George Konig/ Keystone Features), 34 left (National Galleries of Scotland), 34 right (Hulton Archive), 37 left (Hulton Archive), 37 right (English Heritage/ Heritage Images), 38 (National Galleries of Scotland), 40 (Lipnitzki/Roger Viollet), 42 (Hulton Archive), 46 right (The Print Collector), 49 top left (National Galleries of Scotland), 49 bottom left (Mike Marsland/WireImage), 49 right (RKO Radio Pictures), 51 (Hulton Archive), 53 (Waring Abbott), 55 left (Georges Lepape/Conde Nast), 56 left (Melodie Jeng), 56 right (Daniel Zuchnik), 57 right (Jeff J Mitchell), 59 (Archive Photos), 60 right (John Springer Collection/ Corbis), 61 (Michael Ochs Archives), 64 (Sante Forlano/Conde Nast), 65 (Sante Forlano/ Condé Nast), 67 bottom (Tunbridge/Tunbridge-Sedgwick Pictorial Press), 68 (Michael Putland), 75 right (Giancarlo BOTTI/Gamma-Rapho), 79 top left (Edward Berthelot), 79 bottom left (Christian Vierig), 80 (Timur Emek), 83 top (Anwar Hussein/Hulton Archive), 83 bottom left (Kirstin Sinclair), 84 (Education Images/UIG), 87 left (Kirstin Sinclair), 87 bottom right (Georgie Wileman), 89 (Wendy Redfern/Redferns), 90 (Noam Galai/Getty Images for CND), 93 right (Antonio de Moraes Barros Filho/WireImage), 94 (Danny Martindale/WireImage), 96 left (Anthony Harvey), 96 right (Michel Dufour/ WireImage), 99 (Fred Duval/FilmMagic), 101 (Patrick Demarchelier/Conde Nast/Contour by Getty Images), 110 top (George Konig/ Keystone Features), 110 bottom (George Konig/ Keystone Features), 127 top right (Kirstin Sinclair/ FilmMagic), 128 (Sasha), 131 right (Botti/ Gamma-Keystone via Getty Images), 133 left (Sasha), 133 right (Phillips/Topical Press Agency/ Hulton Archive), 134 (Paul Schutzer/The LIFE Premium Collection), 135 (Staff/AFP), 136 (Art Rickerby/The LIFE Picture Collection), 141 (Gerard Julien/AFP), 142 left (PL Gould/ IMAGES), 142 right (Pascal Le Segretain), 152 top right (Timur Emek), 154 (Bettmann), 156 (Nick Harvey/WireImage), 157 (Hulton Archive), 160 bottom (Frances McLaughlin-Gill/Condé Nast via Getty Images), 165 (Rob Stothard), 166 (Lichfield), 169 top left (The Print Collector), 169 bottom left (Hulton Archive), 169 right (W. & D. Downey), 170 left (National Galleries of Scotland), 170 right (Stock Montage), 174 top (SSPL), 174 bottom (SSPL), 175 (Lisa Sheridan/ Hulton Archive), 176 left (Horst P. Horst/ Conde Nast via Getty Images), 179 right (Ray Bellisario/Popperfoto), 181 left (Tim Graham), 181 right (Tim Graham), 182 (Anwar Hussein/ WireImage), 183 (Tim Graham), 188 top (Georgie Wileman), 188 bottom (Kirstin Sinclair), 200 top left (Georgie Wileman), 200 bottom left (Gareth Cattermole), 200 top right (G P Lewis/ IWM via Getty Images), 200 bottom right (Kirstin Sinclair), 202 left (Stuart C. Wilson), 204 left (PYMCA/UIG via Getty Images), 204 bottom right (Venturelli/WireImage), 210 bottom (Bob Chamberlin/Los Angeles Times via Getty Images), 214 top left (Pietro D'Aprano), 214 bottom left (Matthew Sperzel), 214 right (Antonio de Moraes Barros Filho/WireImage), 216 left (Isa Foltin/WireImage), 218 top left (Victor Virgile/ Gamma-Rapho via Getty Images), 218 bottom left (adoc-photos/Corbis), 218 right (Matthew Sperzel), 220 top left (Frank Horvat/Conde Nast via Getty Images), 220 top right (Hulton Archive), 220 bottom right (Frazer Harrison)

Courtesy Lochcarron of Scotland: 199, 201

Ann Martin: 6, 8, 106, 108, 109 left, 109 right, 113 top right, 116, 119 top left, 119 top right, 122, 191, 206

Courtesy Elizabeth Martin, elizabethmartintweed.co.uk: 149 bottom left (Clare Coulter, www.clarecoulter.com)

Courtesy Samantha McCoach/Le Kilt, lekilt.co.uk: 105 left, 105 right

Deirdre McCulloch, www.dmcculloch.com: 114 top, 114 bottom, 125

Courtesy Isaac Mizrahi, www.isaacmizrahi.com: 103

National Museums Scotland: 13, 25

Courtesy New York Public Library: 55 right

Photofest: 41 bottom (Starz), 66, 67 top (Paramount Pictures), 75 left (ABC), 76 (Paramount Pictures)

Courtesy Andrew Rae, www.andrewrae.com, and Roddy Hand, www.rodhand.com: 152 bottom right

Rex/Shutterstock: 10 (Tom Pilston/The Independent), 19 left (Universal History Archive/ Universal Images Group), 44 (Universal History Archive), 57 left (Dan Callister), 58 (Warner Brothers/Everett), 60 left (Everett Collection), 69 (Chris Foster), 71 (Sipa Press), 73 top (Sipa Press), 73 bottom (Press Eye Ltd), 77 (Everett Collection), 79 right (Sipa Press), 83 bottom right (Dvora), 85 (Paul Hartnett/PYMCA), 87 top right (Silvia Olsen), 88 (Mark Ferguson), 93 left (Ken Towner/Associated Newspapers), 131 left (Sharok Hatami), 145 left, 145 top right (Sipa Press), 145 bottom right, 147, 159 left (Glasshouse Images), 160 top left (Associated Newspapers), 162 left (Associated Newspapers), 162 right, 176 right (Everett Collection), 179 left (Sipa Press), 198 left (Sipa Press), 198 top right (Matt Baron/BEI), 202 right (Buzz Foto), 204 top right (Ken Towner/Associated Newspapers), 216 right (David Crump/Associated Newspapers), 220 bottom left (Everett Collection)

Scala Archives: 16 right (Christie's Images, London)

Shutterstock: 1 (stocksolutions), 2-3 (Theodore Trimmer), 4 (Zloneg), 30 (Alessandro Colle), 102 (lev radin), 113 top left (sezer66), 113 bottom (Alex Yeung), 119 bottom (baitong333), 127 bottom left (Carol Blaker), 152 bottom left (Alex Yakimovski), 172 top (Ruth Black), 172 centre (luanateutzi), 172 bottom (stocksolutions), 184 (Nicole Gordine), 187 (Brandon Bourdages), 193 (Hikersmurf), 194 (Anneka), 197 (Brandon Bourdages), 203 (luanateutzi), 205 (Ruth Black), 209 (Goran Bogicevic), 210 top (Helen Cingisiz), 213 (Frank L Junior), 215 (Elena Elisseeva), 217 (Frank L Junior), 219 (luanateutzi), 221 (luanateutzi),237 (Tom Gowanlock), 238-9 (WalterMitty), 240 (Elena Elisseeva)

Courtesy Urgha Loom Shed, urghaloomshed.com: 120, 127 top left, 127 bottom right,

Victoria and Albert Museum, London: 63 (Paul Poiret), 159 right (Frederick Bosworth), 160 top right

Courtesy Walker Slater, www.walkerslater.com: 138 (Gabriela Silveira), 149 bottom right (Gabriela Silveira)

ACKNOWLEDGEMENTS

With thanks to Professor Hugh Cheape of Sabhal MòrOstaig, Dr Sally Tuckett of the University of Glasgow, Julie Lawson and Lucinda Lax of National Portrait Gallery Scotland, Paul Walker and Claire Pentoney of Walker Slater, Maggie Wilson and Georgina Ripley of National Museums Scotland, Lady Anne Dunmore, Caroline de Guitaut of the Royal Collection, Dawn Robson-Bell and Sharon Hart of Lochcarron of Scotland, Hamish and Sheila-Mary Carruthers of Carruthers Associates, Lorna Macaulay and Kristina Macleod of the Harris Tweed Authority, Nick Fiddes of DC Dalgleish, Lynn Wilson of Zero Waste Scotland, David Breckenridge of The Scottish Textile and Leather Association, John McLeish and Peter MacDonald of the Scottish Tartans Authority. Thanks to Nicki Davis at Frances Lincoln for believing in this book and to Sarah Allberrey for designing it so beautifully.

From Ann: To my husband Huw Martin, and my parents Kenneth and Maureen Russell.
From Caroline: To Chris, and to my parents, John and Jill.

Frances Lincoln Limited
74–77 White Lion Street
London N1 9PF
www.quartoknows.com

A catalogue record for this book is available from the British Library.

978-0-7112-3822-0

Printed and bound in China

9 8 7 6 5 4 3 2 1